There can be no other poet like Heather Tosteson, no other who strives so genuinely to take so much into account. She sees "every one of us in this world holding/. . .an enormous universe of feeling," and her lines do not describe this universe but mesh with it. She does not witness the world, she bears it. Hers is the grandest and most honorable ambition, to render without violation "life's silky, staining patina." What an immense revelation *The Sanctity of the Moment* is! How admirable the revealer!
    —Fred Chappell, *Shadow Box, Backsass, Family Gathering, Midquest*, winner of the Bollingen Prize in Poetry, T.S. Eliot Prize, and Aiken Taylor Award.

The Sanctity of the Moment presents the haunting chronicle of a woman/ mother/daughter/lover confronting both the terrible and the beautiful. Dense, intense, and exquisitely formed, these poems, crafted by a brave and unflinching intelligence, teach us much about struggle, compassion and affirmation. There are hard truths contained within these pages—hard truths and unforgettable writing.
    —Kat Meads, *Quizzing the Dead, Sleep, Not Waving*

Heather Tosteson's poems elicit gasps of thankful recognition: I too have struggled with that anger, experienced that joy, felt that despair, known that sadness. Ms. Tosteson's poetic deconstruction of what it means to see the face of God is fearless. In the instant I finished reading *The Sanctity of the Moment*, I believed my life had meaning.
    —Toni Press-Coffman, playwright, *Touch, Stand, We're Here to Help*

THE SANCTITY OF THE MOMENT

THE SANCTITY OF THE MOMENT
Poems from Four Decades

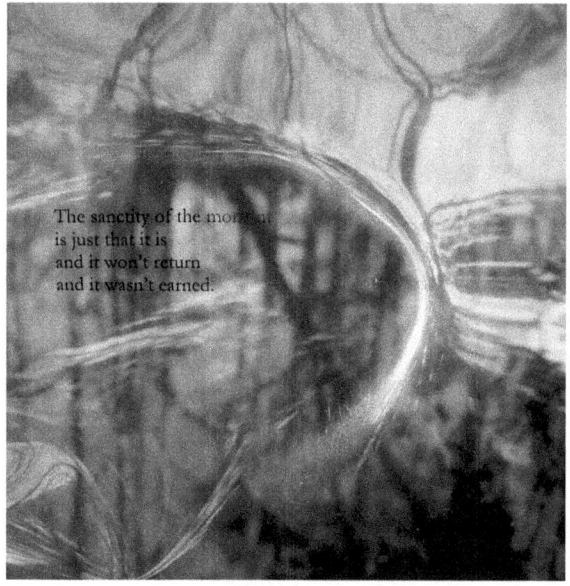

Heather Tosteson

Wising Up Press
Decatur, Georgia

Wising Up Press
P.O. Box 2122
Decatur, GA 30031-2122
www.universaltable.org

Copyright © 2010 by Heather Tosteson

All rights reserved. No part of this book may be used or reproduced in any manner whatsoever without written permission, except in the case of brief quotations embodied in critical articles or reviews.

Catalogue-in-Publication data is on file with the Library of Congress.
LCCN: 2010926563

Wising Up ISBN: 978-0-9796552-9-6

*For Trevor and Charlie,
the two great lasting loves of my life:
for all that you've given,
all that I've received*

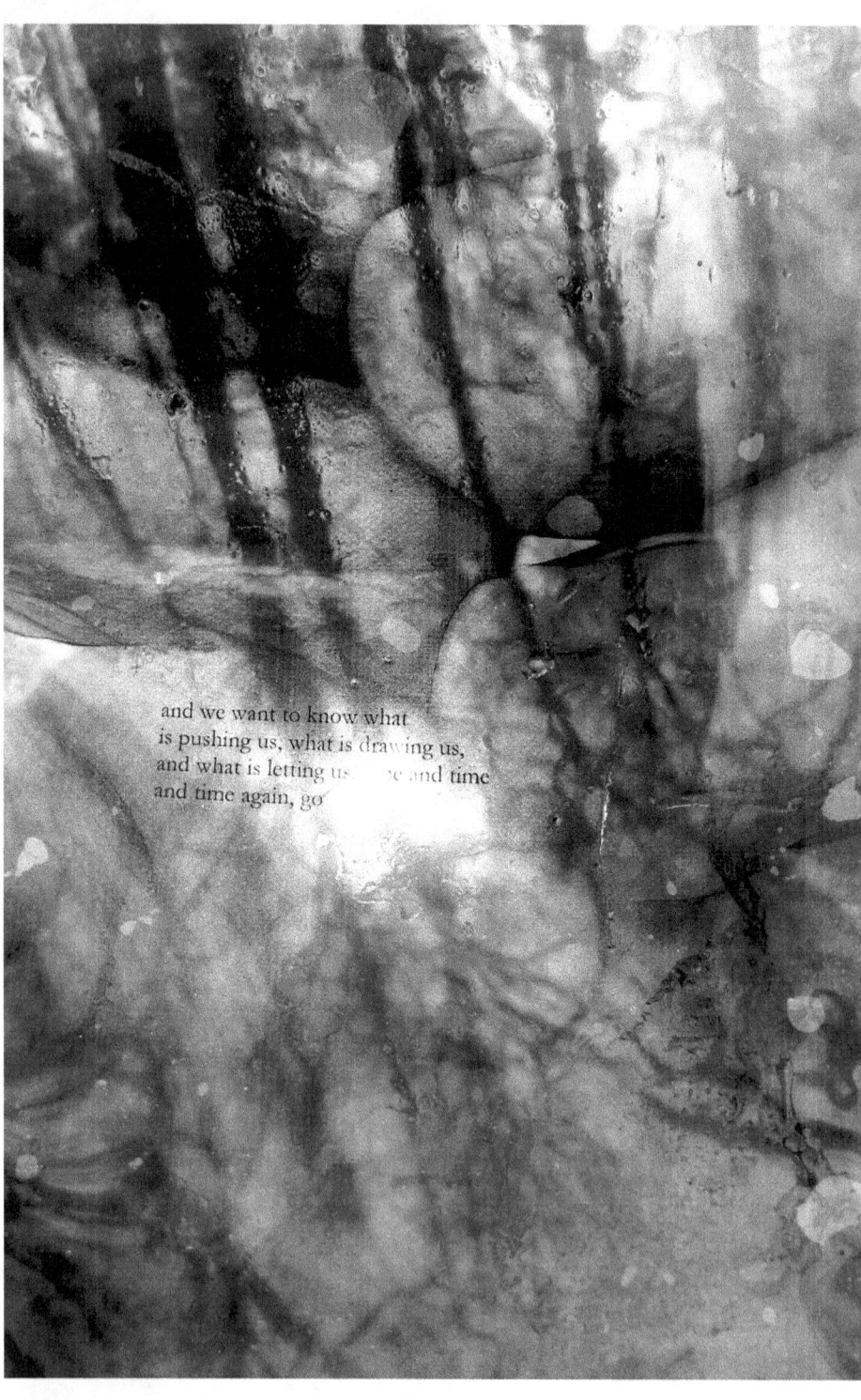

THE SANCTITY OF THE MOMENT
POEMS FROM FOUR DECADES

OVERTURE
Incidence   3

BOOK I : 1970-1979

CAN'T WE JUST BE HAPPY
Passiflora	6
Flux	7
Waltz	8
Home Preserves	9
Can't We Just Be Happy?	10
Maple Seeds	13
Sundew	14
The Fountain	16
Tonight	18
Still Water	19
Lapsed Sonnet	21

SANDSTONE
Mill Street	24
Attendants	25
Dialects	26
January, 1978	28
Civics	31
The Martyr	34
Sandstone	36
Blossom	39
Migraine	43

BOOK II: 1980-1989

MEMBRANES
Clemency	46
Wind	48
Objective Correlatives	52
Glossary	54
Membranes	58
Martinique	61
They Know	64
Teresa	65

BRANDYWINE
Birdnesters	68
Sportsmanship	71
Snow White Rose	76
Heaven	78
Il N'Est Pire Aveugle Que Celui Qui Ne Veut Pas Voir	82
Brandywine	84
Entre L'Arbre et L'Écorce Il Ne Faut Pas Mettre Le Doigt	86

WOMAN DEVOURED BY FISHES
To Welcome Me, You Paint the Walls White	90
Sotano	92
Levin at Fourteen	94
Woman Devoured by Fishes	96
El Día de Los Muertos	100
La Onda	102
I Have Stumbled on Something	104
This Is the Flower	107
If the Image of the Divine in Us Is Our Desire	109

BOOK III: 1990-1999

Reification
Cicatrices	114
Jars	116
Cryptic	119
Spellbound	122
Reification	124

The Intelligence of Loss
Once My Mother Knew My Name	138
The Intelligence of Loss	140
Skin Deep	143
The Call	148
Koan for My Son at Twenty-One	149

Soul House
Así Es	154
Soul House	156
Lexicon	159
Sometimes This Does Not Feel Like Love	165

Faith
Faith	168
Attachment	191
The Sanctity of the Moment	193

BOOK IV: 2000—2009

AUGURY, OMEN

I Am Waiting	196
Sin Titulo	197
Some Silences Are Like Silk	198
There Is a Moment Deep in the Night	200
Shoulder to Shoulder	203
Like Blood in the Vena Cava	204
Brown Recluse	208
Augury, Omen	211
Flight	212
I See Death in My Future	215
Reasonable Expectations	220
Absent-Mindedness	221
Fortunes	223
Burdens	226
It Is What It Is	228
There Is A Story	231
Death Watches	232
We Wait to Be Saved	234
ACKNOWLEDGEMENTS	237
TITLE INDEX	239
AUTHOR	242

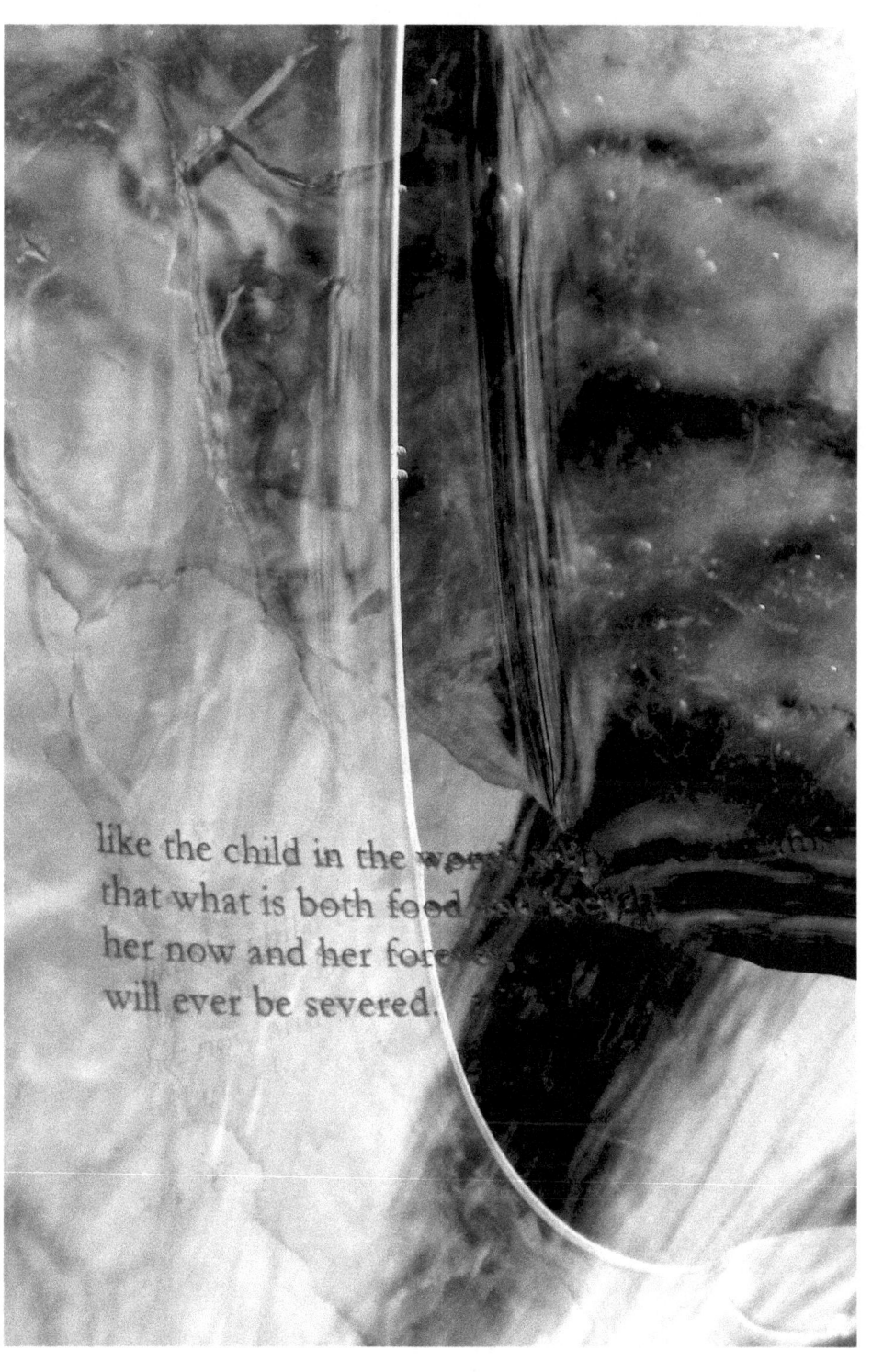

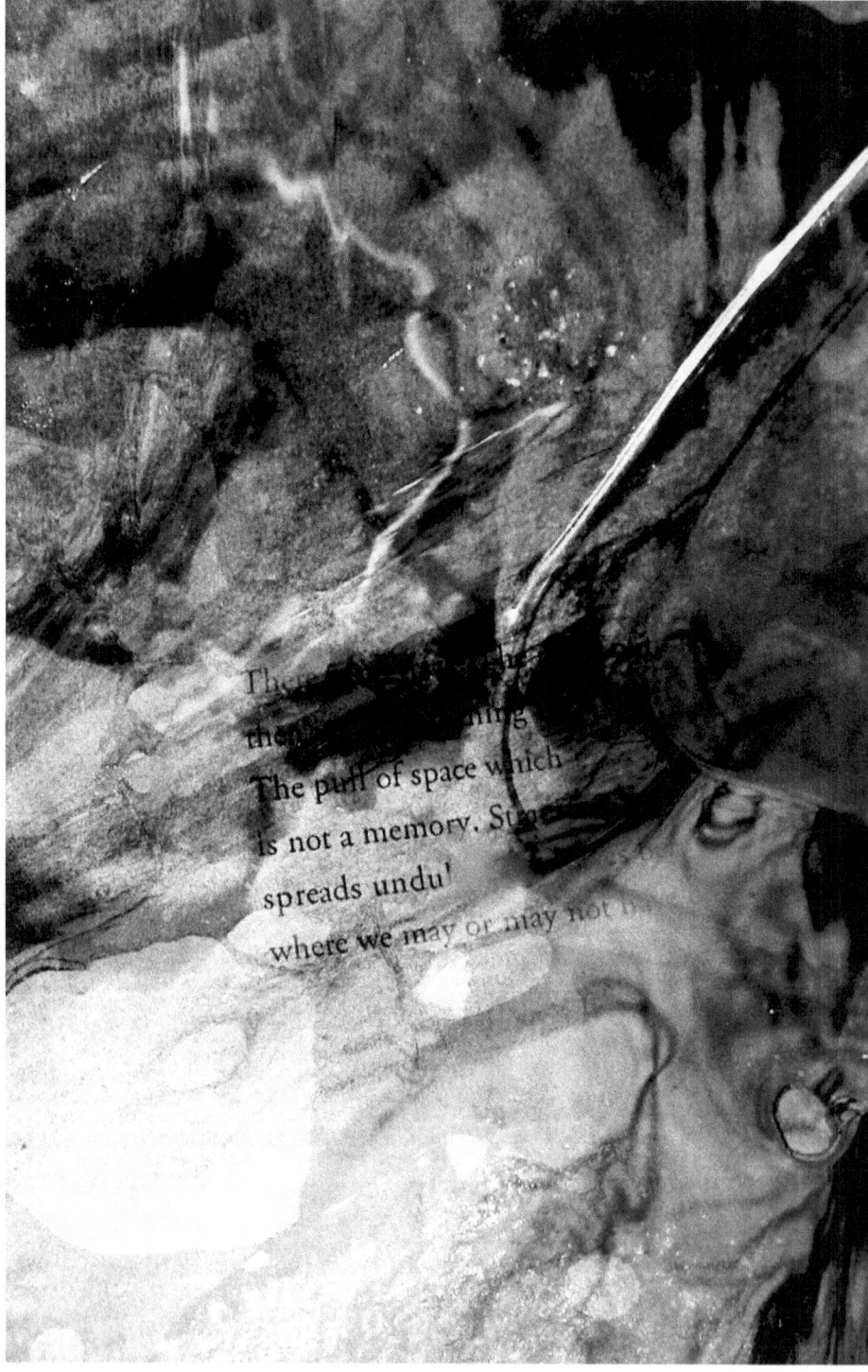

INCIDENCE

The mud flat fuses with the sea,
the sea with the sky.
The swirl of vertigo
rises. A gray surge
which becomes identical sheer
plane, stolid
opacity.
         Against which
the earth exerts actual
suction. Sound: the slap
of sand falling back
into the pools our feet have made.

There is no track. The proof of time
then is in the turning back itself.
The pull of space which realigns
is not a memory. Stranded kelp
spreads undulant red leaves before us
where we may or may not have been.

BOOK I: 1970-1979
I
CAN'T WE JUST BE HAPPY

PASSIFLORA

Late summer, out on the balcony, late
evening, the sky was the color of ripe apricots.
All women do, I thought, is wait, watch.
For what? Sixteen, I waited for dusk, dark.

In Farmer Crabtree's far acre, a gray mule browsed.
Its tail, tattered broom, swept away time.
Far off on the highway, cars sounded like fire.
All women do, I thought, is weep. Why?

Rasp of gravel, dull thud of door after door,
and then, through glass, the bickering, a dull
murmur, like a dog worrying at a bur.
The sky was the color of oak bark.

All women do, I thought, is watch.
Sixteen, and still to me their faces loomed
larger than life, actors in a baffling movie.
All a girl does to turn, I thought, is wait.

For what? I was green wood—
even in dream, hip and breast untouched.
All I want to do, I thought, is escape.
Far off, on the highway, cars sounded like wind.

If I stay thin, I thought, and rocked myself to sleep.
Late summer, the land was too green. I began to dream
of frail red cedars breathless under shrouds of kudzu.
I began to dream of Farmer Crabtree's scythe.

FLUX

As a child, after the stories, the songs,
the lights flicked out, screams would flood
our house. I trusted them. I saved terror
for the silence that drew me out of bed, up
the stairs, for the thick white hands, flaccid
with drink, that slowly culled the stem,
the bowl of a shattered glass.

We never knew if the pieces fit. The hands
would always miss. And still we watched,
all of us as lost inside ourselves as she was,
the tedious attempts. It seemed they would never end.
But, of course, they did. And, when the hands
stopped, curled up on the table like small
dead animals, we knew what it meant.

The house was a sealed jar.
We would have to leave, or so we thought,
and lived on in that place for years.
Like smoke from damp wood, the air
we shared was thick and warm and dark
and filled with oxygen.
Obviously. It is difficult to accept.

Bitter, sweet, somber—these words last
as long as it takes to say them.
Breathing in again, our lungs accept everything:
dust, smoke, snow, the smell of dried
tarragon or spilled gasoline, the smell of our own
breath, human passion, human fear, sweat.

WALTZ

We dance without passion but the movement
is reminiscent and I could follow you,
if I chose, with my eyes closed. I lay one finger
on your cheek like a scar. Your skin is white, cool.
I have never wounded you, although once
I wanted to. Tonight I enjoy the fine,
unmarred texture of your skin and the ease
with which you embrace me. How delicately
we touch the ones we do not love.
I can feel the convulsion begin, the raw edges
of a wound moving like a mouth in speech.
I turn away and my gesture is formless,
awkward, the movement of a prehistoric fish
dredged up and exposed to light for the first time.

HOME PRESERVES

Time doesn't pass. One summer,
this one, having completed the last
of my chores each morning, I close
my kitchen cabinets on whole shelves
I've stocked with sealed mason jars.

Only tomatoes preserved in salted water
retain their own shape, color.
I close the doors on that flesh
just beginning to loosen, that brine

only slightly tinted red, and see
as my arm descends, a woman
standing alone on the verge of a town
that has gone up in flames behind her.

Like Cassandra she stands with one arm upraised—
and like Cassandra her mind is opened up behind.
Inside her open mouth the flames are dancing
like many tongues. I will not listen.

CAN'T WE JUST BE HAPPY

"Can't we just be happy and watch
T.V.?" you ask. You empty the last
of a fifth of scotch in your glass.
"Why are you doing this to me?"
What can I say? I'm sorry?
I'm frightened? I want to be
a good, loyal wife, but death
keeps making advances
and my resolve is weakening?
When he comes up behind me
in the shower and kisses
the nape of my neck, I shudder
with pleasure? The hand which
covers mine and helps me guide
the razor is more tender
and comforting than yours?
I'm obsessed with desire
for a single bed? "Can't we
just be happy?" you ask.

I put you to bed with your bottle.
The baby is safely sleeping with his bear.
I wash the dinner dishes. My hand
doubles as whetstone. I sharpen
paring knives and meat cleavers.
Lately, all my dreams are blatant
wishes. Only last night I admitted
I was sick. You showed
remarkable compassion. You chose

not to love me. I woke laughing.
I resent this embryo growing
inside me. It is a cancer
about which I'm not free to speak.
As you said, you never expected
to hear the mother of your son
say something like that.

"Why are you doing this to me?
Can't we just watch T.V. and be happy?"
Death puts his tongue in my ear.
The knife slips. What can I say?
I'm sorry. It was an accident.

MAPLE SEEDS

It is an absolutely tranquil picture.
You caught each warp in the maple
seeds, the liquid fall of the leaves,
the tinge of red in the veins.
You always kept your lens immaculate.
The eye you turned to nature
was immaculate. You saw purely
in terms of color and symmetry.
I had unlimited respect for your detachment.
At the zoo you could catch animals
in the most impressive poses.
No one would have known they weren't
in their native habitats, that you'd
stood there for hours, your camera
focused exactly between two bars, waiting
for a panda to enter your field of vision.
You photographed your son in the same way.
I'm sure, having chosen never to see
him again, you'll remember him always
as you saw him then. On walks, the two
of us silent as usual, you'd turn and catch
the child in such a way his hair
became the sun and his skin seemed
translucent, almost ethereal, blue.

SUNDEW

Of course I couldn't leave the sundew,
that bloodshot lidless eye. Although for years
it has hung over my head to protect
me while I slept, lately I've moved it,
placed it opposite my bed. The backdrop
is a briny black. You focused
so closely on that carnivorous plant
it became an abstract spiral of green
mouths and red spines. The viscous
liquid secreted to snare insects
is dew, fresh dew. A dandelion
gone to seed is a cameo woman.
She extends like a figurehead
over the prow of those mouths, the gush
of blood, the grass, the one drowned
fly. If I stare down into the center
of the plant where the mouths are all opening,
the grass blades at the lower left corner
keep drawing my eye down and back up
to the woman, a marble silhouette.
The plant meant nothing to you.
To me it was a picture of hatred.
An eye that would never shut.
It protected me when you invaded my dreams:
I would hear a scuffling and run
to my son's room and see you
scrabbling at the screen.
You were coming to take him.
You looked up at me. The edges
of your mouth were slack and wet

with liquor. You had a special smile for those
occasions. A complex blend of shame and the most
intense will. I would shake my head.
I would stare until your face dissolved
into an abstract composition of red lips, sallow
green skin: your face in the morning
when I saw you casually dusting
at the insecticide you'd spilled in a child's
library book. "Go ahead and take it back.
If they don't know it won't hurt them."
But by then the dream had ended. I was awake
and safe. The locks were all in place.
The only sounds were my son's soft breathing,
the gray rain beating on the dusty panes.

THE FOUNTAIN

My favorite, the fountain in the garden,
you never framed. I liked that.
It meant I could prop it on my desk.
I could touch it. It is a scene
from a place I knew before I knew you.
You photographed it at an odd angle,
but I know how it should be,
how it appeared to me when I was sixteen.
It is a small, stagnant pond where irises
grow in the spring, yellow and purple
lotuses bloom in the summer. In the center
of the green leaves, the algae covered water,
there is an iron birdbath, or fountain.
The basin brims with deep red water.
It is an extremely quiet place. Ten feet
away there is a solid screen of magnolias.
The photograph only catches the lower branches,
and the long shadows. But the park
is as familiar to me as my own heart
so I know behind the trees there stands
a statue of a soldier sowing grain. I forget,
but I think it's a memorial to the end of a war.

as you watched him then, as we'd... the two
of us silent as usual, you'd turn and catch
the child in such a way his hair
became the sun and his skin seemed
translucent, almost ethereal, blue.

TONIGHT

dogs are out hunting the caved
moon. In her lair she is turning
to attack. I hear your voice
draw back, draw back. 2 A.M.
I can't get the dogs to stop
baying. I leap to grip
that dark disc, absence,
and turn it round—
only to wake fettered to this bed,
this house you've never entered,
this town where at dawn chained
dogs yawn, trains begin to howl.

STILL WATER

I've come here hoping to see your face
again. Instead, you appear at the edge
of the forest behind me, dressed
in your silver gown, calling,
"Come dance, come dance, my darling."
The moon erodes on the river.

Grandmother, I have found a silver lover.
He covers me like your gown.
I am trapped in a circle of light.
I'm green at this. I want to be beside
it all, cloud on the moon's face,
a thorn imbedded in its eye.
I want to stay here with you.

Grandmother, the moon is a pared nail.
It won't disappear. My shadow
keeps surfacing like a man
ten days drowned. You're dead
and have been dead a year—
but your voice wells from the trees
each night calling me to dance, to dance.

Was this your gift? Your voice
like a hand on my shoulder forces
me to turn from your face, blank
river, and to find in that inexhaustible
light which falls through an arch
of black leaves each night the threat
of solace. How could you? I was content.

...between the brown ...
... lace, in small red ca...
...ve could stay the moment whe...

its reflection meet, when wa...

As it is we can't breathe...

...r the hand the plucked da...

...en, with one lift of w...

LAPSED SONNET

After the first frost, the air is burdened
with light. The wings of gnats and bees thicken.
They hover, now, in the spaces between green
blades of grass, between the brown ribs of dead
Queen Anne's lace, in small red caves in the clover.
Listen: if we could stay the moment when the bent
maple and its reflection meet, when water is leaf
and both...As it is we can't breathe
or touch. In the hand the plucked dandelion
is luminous—then, with one lilt of wind,
the bright galaxy collapses, and we, I confess, breathe
more freely watching the last dull gray filament
drift across the surface of our palm.

                                          Listen—
if we could admit last night we both drew equal
sustenance from the cold night air, the distance
between us, between us and the stars—
if we could admit we choose to chart
our way by fixed constellations, who
would blame us? Orion? The Bear?
Light, your hand on your collar, turning into light, turning
away. A moment, I confess, I thought of those tremulous
planets, Venus and Mars.

II
SANDSTONE

MILL STREET

Women see the world too much through glass—old
wives' tale. Around here young mothers leave
their curtains shut all day. If you asked them,
lives, they would explain, are lived inside
cinder blocks, thick curtains, smudged glass.

I think they speak the truth. Listen, in the summer,
in the evening, when fighting the heat, they leave
open their windows and doors—the air rocks
with gunshots and lullabyes and children's sobs.

Even on winter nights when all the homes are sealed,
through walls you hear children gibbering
in their baths, and later, the voices of their mothers
and fathers, shunted through radiator pipes, falter
like a pulse. Their quarrels echo in my quiet house.

I find the sounds soothing as sweeping the floor,
marking each day off the calendar,
or sleeping alone.

ATTENDANTS

With eyes big as lemurs', the men are the dreamers around here. You can see them, fists thrust deep into pockets, standing at their storm doors in the evening, their breath smogging the glass. Harshly, they ask their wives for rags.

Or at least one does, an American, who lives opposite me in apartment K-10. I can read his lips, read too the movements of his young wife, her blonde hair drawn back in despair, straightening pictures, knocking the dust out of pillows, her mouth open, her body screaming, Look at me, LOOK AT ME.

The man in K-10 doesn't listen. He looks at me—late at night, returning from the laundromat, or beating my rugs on the railing of the balcony. He imagines it would all be different over here. He thinks I am lonely. He thinks I too want to leave these apartments—for a husband, a house.

The dreams of the man in K-10 are different in kind from the dreams of the man in C-9. But he too stands at his door and stares at me because I am unmarried. Walking with my son once, I saw him in a knot of men all talking a language I can't understand. He nodded directly at me, said something, and laughed. Then he and his friends sat to watch us pass. They made me feel like an empty room. They made me want to go straight home and scour myself out.

Because the man in C-9 won't stop following me with his eyes, in self-protection I have made friends with his child and his pregnant wife. When we meet at the laundromat, we mime our feelings about broken washing machines, about folding mounds of laundry. I know like me she loves her son. I have no idea what she dreams. But I think she probably feels less betrayed than the woman in K-10.

[25]

DIALECTS

i

Fists clenched, a man, decked in a steel blue suit, backs across the grass. Slowly, the swarthy young man follows, heaving his bare arms out. Up. Astonishing, the weight of air in arguments, the torpor of the body just before the torso twists and the leg, effortless, extends—

Far above us, two Brazilian women stop and rest their arms on the railing of the balcony. They watch, their faces slack, as if in great fatigue or boredom. Fist and fist. One red rose blooms just above a rust-colored beard.

Furious clatter of heels, lash of glossy black hair—in between the men glides an exquisite young woman. Grabbing both her husband's hands in one of hers, she harangues the other man in Spanish. She stamps her foot. Twice, thoughtlessly, she draws her hand, his, up and down her hip—

For a second, I can imagine their bodies during love. Anxious, I look off, up. The Brazilian women wave and smile with innocent pleasure. The last scene in the afternoon matinee. Rhapsodic, my son cries, *Men!* He shadow-boxes all the way home.

ii

"Aw, you wanna fight? All right. Let's go." My brother moves toward the crowd of sixth-graders. He is six and I am eight. Restless, I edge back but keep a firm grip on his shirt. Oh, I think, what if I get sick on the sidewalk? He's got to get us out of this, he got us in. My brother keeps talking, talking, talking. Slowly, their faces relax, they laugh, and, vanquished, herd off like sheep.

"Can't you talk?" Twelve years old, for two whole days, he sat cross-legged on the edge of his bed, burning Vitalis for its blue flame.

"Maybe I can—" Even the dark couldn't blur that look.

"Back off." And then he began to talk. "Ass. He was a bloody ass. I kept pounding his head on the floor of the bus. My mind went black. The time I learned about the universe—it was like that. Can you understand?"

iii

"All right," I say, twenty-five and quite mad in my own right with loss. "Try men. You have to love someone."

"No," my brother answers. "The only people I love less than women are men. And," he adds, "it is reprehensible to touch anything you don't care for."

Angelic, almost, the outline of his face as he slouches back in his chair and laughs. I have never known so sane—or chaste—a hatred.

"Coward," I said, and then, short of breath, tackled the boy. Over and over, I heard his head thud on the grass. "Take it back."

Men came running. "Too old, too old," they scolded. I was thirteen, and mad. "But he called me fat!" Which I was, and miserable, and a little bit in love, although I could never have named it.

I liked, you see, the weight of his head inside my hand, the way his blonde hair shimmered on my wrist, the way my own skin, as if I'd been in the sun too long, felt flushed and tender.

JANUARY, 1978

It is a question of wanting an entirely new thing, of undertaking a kind of renovation of yourself, in all simplicity, with the fixed idea: ça ira.
                                            Vincent Van Gogh

This evening you come home singing.
On your sled, snagged between the boards,
an ornate branch. All through dinner
we turn and turn the vase, testing
perspectives. I say,
no, it is too close
to my eyes—
            but, suddenly, looking through
the branches, one thorn almost brushing
my eyelid, I see an infinite
purity of gray
            thorn gray
                        branch white
wall.

You come up behind me. Your tongue
leaves snail tracks on my cheek.
You laugh and tell me, "Lions
love like this." Then you sing,
parodying the radio:
I love the cherry branch.
I love the cherry.
I love the brown cherry stone.
I join the chorus, and you join me
as I take the branch up to my room.

At night now, magnified by moonlight,
it covers my bedroom wall like script
I cannot read yet. I try to accept that
as I do the ice moving in terrifying
puzzles on the river outside my window,
as I do your mysterious sources
of knowledge. "Did you know,"
you call out at midnight, "dinosaurs
have little picks on their feet
so walking in the snow they won't fall?"

CIVICS

Drawn by an unfamiliar trill
in our children's voices,
we stand at our storm doors and stare
down into the courtyard where
the children glide like kites
through the cold white winter twilight.

Fire! Fire!
cry Trevor and Tope, Scott and Moriah.

And then, Brazilian and Saudi,
American and Sudanese, leaning
over balconies, clinging to the stair rails,
we hear our own voices ricochet:
What's that you say say say

Fire! Fire!
cry Trevor and Tope, Scott and Moriah.
Running toward us, their arms drift
back on the wind like thin silk banners.
Higher, they say, higher.

Flames weave bright as hibiscus
in and out of the balustrade.
Four Nigerian men enter in pairs
from an unlit hall, and, calmly
raising their arms to shield
their eyes, bend to inspect the fire.
Their faces dwindle in the dusk.

And now the flames too look small, dull
tendrils of a dying vine. But behind
the men their shadows rise
to form another image, antiphonal,
obscure, that draws from all of us
a sigh of fear.

Corinne,
resting her back against the lamppost
raises her eyes and then, like a sullen
madonna, she grips her son Scott to her breast and tips
his face up: *What's
burning?*

But the children,
in voices to which the chill
March twilight gives an eerie
density, call us back
to sectless and earthly communions.

Why won't the fire stop? asks Scott.
Who's to blame? wonder mothers and fathers.
I know his name, says Moriah.
Now you stay back, I say to Trevor.
The air is acrid with hot metal, charred rubber.

I dial the fire department.
A murmur of amazement eddies
among black women wrapped in calico
as they hear the sirens echo
against the low hills of Southern Ohio.

Oh no. Oh no, my son moans.
There's no fire anymore.
In the darkening air, his face
looks round and white
with fear. Hide,
he whispers. The cops
will lock you up for joking.

THE MARTYR

He was tall and thin and we never saw him smiling.
He had a son named Tim whom he always kept beside him.
When he lived in our courtyard, the grim self-
congratulatory expression with which he walked
his kid, or shouldered the burden of the garbage,
earned him his nickname, The Martyr.
That was before we came, before his wife left,
and he moved into the high-rise restricted
to the childless. His son slept on the couch
under windows screened day in day out
with philodendron and wandering jew, a cloth
so thick only the children, accustomed
to tunneling through bright berried hedgerows,
thought to peer through. "The air
in there," my son told me, "is blue, and quiet
as night. When his dad's not looking, Tim
waves at me. I think we're going to run away
together and make our fortunes."
That was the year my son loved money more
than his mother, brooded over the myth
of Midas (if the fork had been longer,
he wondered, and the king had bad
table manners...), the year he slept
with a green felt bag of tarnished
Mardi Gras coins tucked under his pillow.

"Are these yours?" the Martyr, looming
at our doorway one evening, opened his fist
and showed me three gold coins. "Tim says

he found them on the windowsill and he's sure
they're a present." I nodded. "I wanted to check.
I don't want my kid to steal." "Maybe,"
I said, "your kid was just being honest." My face
felt as taut as his. "In any case, my kid
won't miss them. He can't count yet." Without
another word, the father closed his hand,
turned on his heel. "What's that man like?"
I asked my son when he came in for the night.
"Is he mean to Tim?" "He's like," he said, parroting
my worst fear, "like you." "I know," I said,
toweling him dry, "that you left the coins—but why?"
"We thought if we left them out in the sun
and poured water on them, they might grow like seeds."
I handed him his green bag. He tucked it back
under his pillow, "Then," he said sleepily,
"he could have lots and lots of money without leaving home."

SANDSTONE

Simple things can leave me speechless—the shifting color
in a sandstone cliff, the shapes of cinders, the way each
leaf in the wall of trees across the Hocking turns differently,
the way wind shatters light, patterns it, differently each morning.
I fear we live, as we can't live, without analogy.
How can I explain then the way we listen to each other
here in Mill Street? Stories pass among us like cups of sugar,
cannisters of flour, our children's jumpropes, softballs and bats.
Some stories are gossip and easy to forget, but
some of them are attempts at exorcism. "Did you hear?"

Through her kitchen window, Maureen and I watched our children,
their backs the color of dead grass, but luminous, swing, belly
down, on the playground below us, their feet digging ridges
in the dust. Summer, air heavy as dust, morning trains sound
like thunder. "When you were gone…did you hear?" A neighbor,
at midnight, had come storming out of his house. His wife,
calling after him, came too and stood, sobbing, in the courtyard.
Maureen, out on the balcony because she couldn't sleep,
asked if she could help. You see, here we're all young, everyone
has children, and marriage is as difficult as it will
ever be. But the woman, shaking her head, said, "God help us.
They're beating a child over there. We can see the shadows
on our wall. It's been going on for hours." The morning train
is gone, and Maureen turns to me, the light on her face brighter
than her daughter's hair. "I was out there because the child's screams
were so loud I thought he was outside my door. He was three
buildings away." Maureen's voice is calm, but her hand trembles
as she turns to the stove. To think back on it as I write
is like touching her cheek, like watching shadows.

                              But the dull
flush that rises over my son's back after I've spanked him,
the bright rose that blooms in Beth's cheek when she's screamed at—
what name?

"It's just that their skin is so goddamn thin," I snapped at a friend
who has no children, believes in discipline, and thinks anger
can be forgiven. Perhaps it can. But I've seen my son's
eyes darken like water when a cloud covers the sun, worse
than tears, the way he touches my stinging palm—and nods
as if he understood as he understands that his god
as a bad god because he kills people, his god is good
and fit to be worshipped, is power, that families live
forever, and, oh yes, turning in the doorway when he was three,
"You mean we're all going to die. We will each be so unhappy."

BLOSSOM

In a clamor of voices and drums,
                           the heat-stunned crowd
wheels
like a drowsed beast round
                   round
                          round the pavilion.

My son sits on the edge of the stage
and shakes his head in time.
                          The man behind me clamps
my shoulder, draws close, and hisses—
something.

We near the stage,
         my son leans forward,
                          I break free.
"I think I want to go home," he mutters.

Hands clasped, stock still,
we eye the dizzying spiral.
                 Man and woman,
sometimes it seems we're all figures on Keats' vase,
reaching out not for truth or beauty, but the simple
satisfaction of the flesh.
             O happy happy lust

As if the satisfaction of the flesh were...
                          Peter
heads the writhing line. Peter...Ah!
                          He's the one
who climbs Anne's balcony and peers
             in the window when David is with her.

                              What in hell
are you after? she asks him.
                         And he says—
                                        Marriage.

   O happy happy

            Out of the gleaming bowl, the drummer beats
with muffled sticks a melody.
                 Karen waves and shimmies by.
                                 "Even I," a friend said,
touching his thick farmer's hand nervously to his forehead,
"have slept with more women this year than—"
                                         Alley Cat.
Night Train.

A woman grabs my hand and drags me back into the ring.
My son waves.
            Even at a distance, he looks scared.
                              Perhaps for him the laughter
and catcalls of the crowd, the slap
of bare feet on the concrete floor, the incessant belling
of the drums, all
                have the quality of nightmare.

                                 This time around,
I'm happy, snared
            by the music, the motion.
                              "This time around,"
I said to my last lover, "I won't bother
         to give it a name. Because," I added,
                              "if I believed each
failure to love brings you one ring nearer the center
of hell,
            then I'm dangerously close to eternal damnation now."

I saw the look on his face and quickly said,
                              "*If*
I believed—"

              Under the bright lights, the drummers' skins
gleam blue.
              The face of the woman ahead of me flushes.
The man behind me cups my shoulder in his damp palm.

—That night
           I saw under his skin the heart moving
like some undulant animal.
                        And the way his breath never
quickened even at the height of passion made me think
at the center of desire
              one might find…
                                    A thought
lost now in the clatter of drums,
                        the sough of wind
through thin skirts.

                    Leaving the pavilion, I pause
                              to watch the dancers,
scattered over the dark hillside,
                    spiral,
                              as we have done,
into
     and out of
                    that dark core of music.
                              On the verge

of the wood two lovers lie down. The woman's white skirt
bright and senseless as the stars, still whirls and burns.

MIGRAINE

The one blackbird in the mulberry tree
hops from branch to branch.
My child, sleeping restlessly, hears berries
fall incessantly, an echo
of the blood thudding inside his skull.

My sleeping child shifts restlessly.
The sky is turning purple. His dreams
darken like bruises. Fear rustles
through our empty house, incessant
as his cry: "Where are we moving this time? Why?"

> ...ouches the...
> ...slick and tremulo[us]
> ...hollows and bells in...
> Like every God-forsaken th[ing]
> it too sings with light.

BOOK II: 1980-1989
I
MEMBRANES

CLEMENCY

Lilies, immaculate and cool as fallen moons,
gleam in the shadows of the eucalyptus,
while, on the sheer green cliffs, hundreds
of sea poppies burn and wink and burn again
like that much more celestial litter.

This land is an ascetic's nightmare.

Here even the petals of the iris
have the eerie solidity of an eyelid,
here even the chaste body holds
the odor of birth.

Waking, I share the stunned
fear of the faithless. How can I go on
knowing the one landscape
I have a carried a lifetime inside me
like a knowledge of God has been denied?

I buy time: I walk the sere beach,
collect the cleft, sea-scoured shells,
and, returning, arrange and rearrange
them on my brilliant sills.

Reminded by this, the heart calms.
Joy remains what it has always been,
a scavenger.

Then the sun touches the bed, and again
the flesh, slick and tremulous as liquid
glass, hollows and bells in the wind.

Like every God-forsaken thing in the universe,
it too sings with light.

WIND

i

What form can hold this evening in January, the storm
whirling in over the dark Pacific, the chimney's wail,
the weak cry of the floorboards under the deliberate
tread of a child who, candle gripped tenuously
between forefinger and thumb, threads a dark hall,
bears the face of an old man, and calls out
to no one.

ii

All night the wind screamed like a flock of gulls.
The windows rattled in their rotten sills, the house rocked
like an ark. The storm: flurry of gray wings, sharp
beaks, bright yellow eyes, torn—

I am afraid, of course, to say more.
The mind exists behind the senses,
and behind the mind,
language.

iii

What story can we write that doesn't begin:
First…and then…and then…and then.
Even in the dark, the mind dark, we insist.
The gulls descend because they are hungry,
the sea beats against the land,
a gray-robed mother in frenzied grief,
a stricken beast.

All night the stories are told.
Rocked in the white hollow of a wave,
the red belly of a whale,
the resinous hold of a ship,
we listen attentive and faithful as children.

We wake no wiser.
For who among us has the strength to say
we have tossed in our beds aimlessly
tormented?

iv

We are always setting new disciplines for the eye
and the heart, otherwise we forget
the past is a labyrinth.
We forget the frail luminous woman
who, deep within the slick cold tunnel,
holds out to us the cupped flame, our names
spinning like a bright thread from her lips,
is death. Life is the sick beast bellowing.

v

After a storm, the world feels preternaturally still.
An old man clangs the door to his back porch.
The sea and sky pale. The lights die. Time
is the eye's movement between two points in space.

The old man stretches, take off his glasses, looks up
at the sky and smiles. A terrier winds like a hungry cat
between his legs as he descends the sagging stairs,
threads his way through a maze of broken
lilies, broken tiles.

Above him, on a peaked red roof, a pigeon preens
and preens its iridescent neck, its dull wet back.
My son's voice, resonant as dove's, fills the room.
In the hollows in the plaster, like a dun spray of roses,
fungi bloom. Conception is one definition of love.

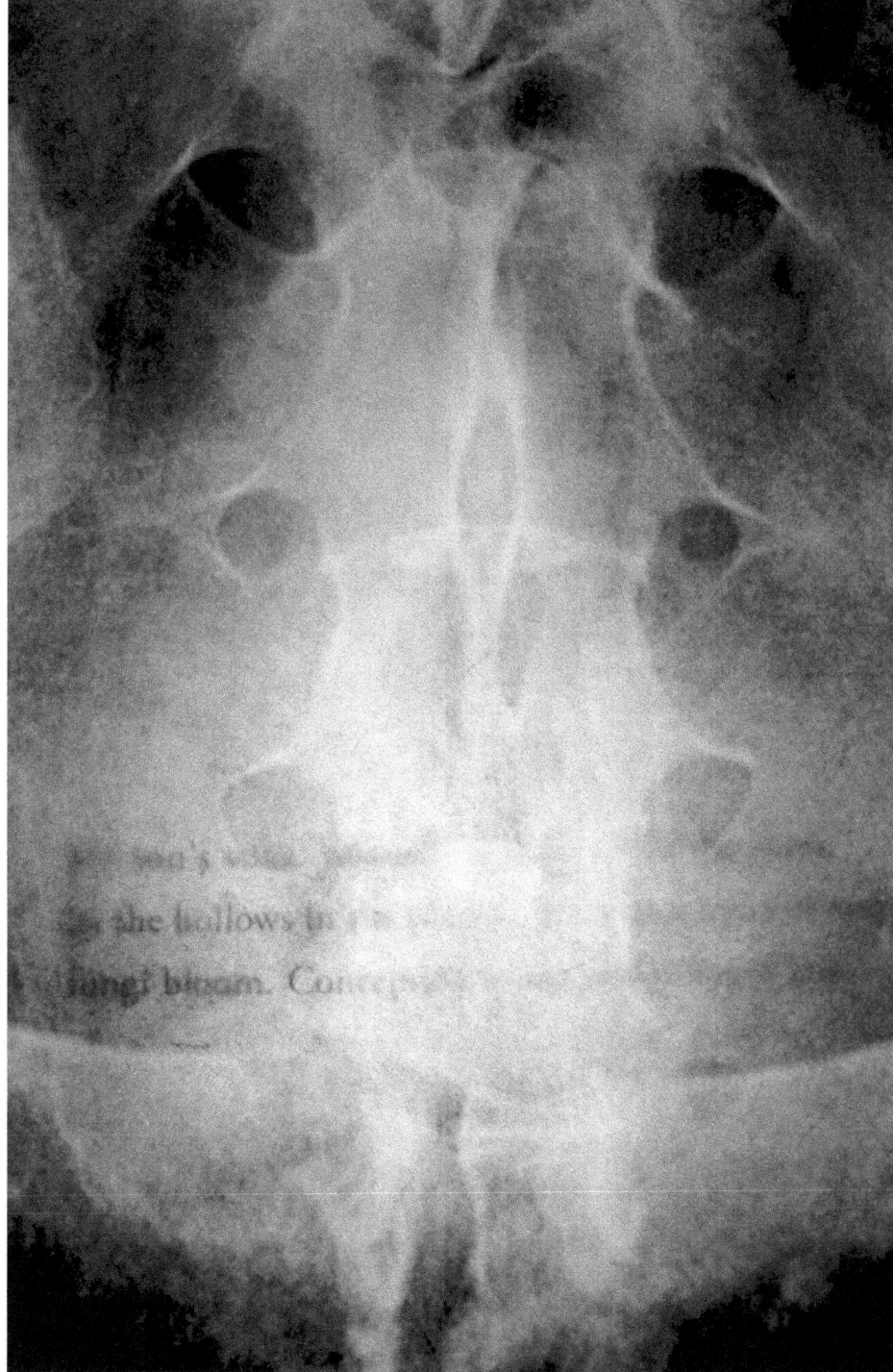

OBJECTIVE CORRELATIVES

Under the eaves
of the Chinese Seventh Day Adventist church,
a young woman, smoking
a cigarette with mechanical
insouciance, waits for the Geary express.

Kneeling on the sidewalk, a small boy
methodically dries, with a tattered white
tissue, the inside of his big black umbrella.
He pauses, peers through misted
glasses, then rubs again in long
swatches from spoke to spoke.

Watching the child preen, with silent
deliberation, the dark spread wing
that has shadowed his dreams for weeks,
the young woman, still in the strutted
stance of a dancer, suddenly
understands the flesh will always be heavy
as water that can't rise, light
as water that can't fall.

Somewhere deep inside this city
in a muddle of dull green vines,
bright blue trumpets sound, morning
glories.

"Look," he says, breaking
a branch from a flowering bush,
the needles inside his palm, holding
them to his face, breathing—

"They forgot to give
his one a sign."

GLOSSARY

i

I don't know what they do—Feverfew, Motherwort, Rue—
but I can imagine, as I can't imagine the use of elecampane.
I write it down. Writing is a technology, or so say priests
and linguists. I sound the cymbals I have made.
El-e-cam-pane. I sound another sequence
of syllables—chamomile—another—lungwort—and feel
the gray bag inside me billow, flatten, billow.

ii

Comfrey.

On a grass-stained pad of graph paper, my son slowly
copies down the word. He yawns uncontrollably.
He always does when he tries to read or write. The symbols
themselves give him difficulty. He can't see the difference
between a W or M, a P or 9. *Wormswood*
he writes, checking it twice against the sign.

iii

Sky. Is. Fall.
These words written were my weapons
and I shot them nightly from my arched tongue.

For terror, in my seventh year, was substantial,
an animal.

With a tread regular as my own pulse, it stalked
a house so still it felt like there was no one left
inside it breathing. Except for me.

I knew the animal was insatiable as me.

And I knew, unlike me, it could groan and die
and come right back
to life.

iv

YOU LET ME BE, he screams at night, mastering
a line from his first reader.
Seven, he makes his weapons out of cardboard
or warped plywood. On reels of brown paper
we've tacked to the walls, he draws diagrams,
then quietly studies the anatomy of his dreams.

Clary he writes now and hands me the notebook
to copy *Scolopendrium*.

v

Now read me, he demands, what we've written.
*Comfrey, wormswood, feverfew, rue,
motherwort*—

Three times he headed out, three times he stopped—
hearing what? The shirr of wheels on damp
asphalt? The screech of a rusted axle?
When at last he reached the far curb,
he looked up, saw me at the window, waved,
and, with a little hop, disappeared around the corner.

Go on, he says, shaking the paper.
You haven't finished the reading yet.
Scolopendrium and *chamomile. Lungwort.*

This morning, waving to him, closing
the window, I kept saying his given
name over and over under
my breath.

vi

Lying in bed last night, he drew a supine monster big
and fat and grinning like a Cheshire cat. It has a little
hole above its left clavicle where the air comes in and
fills a big balloon. When the balloon is full, it jostles
a little man who jostles a little octopus. The octopus
lets loose some dark chemicals that the man collects
in his hands and puts back in the balloon. When the balloon
collapses, the man edges away from the octopus;
the octopus stretches its tentacles, yawns, and goes back
to sleep. This process, he assures me, is not the way his
nice monster speaks. It speaks by twanging rubber bands.

vii

Look, he says, breaking
a branch from a flowering bush, crushing
the needles inside his palm, holding
them to his face, breathing—

"They forgot to give
this one a sign."

On days like this I can't
touch him—*my*
elecampane.

MEMBRANES

This morning the rain screens the open
window, empty doorway, an afterthought
that, like the blood in our veins, is always leaving,
arriving, always there.
We hear it when we close the door.

It isn't a question of solitude
or the heart gaping like an infant's mouth for food.
It isn't a question.
I *can't always be looking behind me.*

Rain creates, admit it, a delicious tedium.
Unsettled by the cool drift of silt, the bird's erratic
caterwaul, the hum of electricity, the breath
of the man in the next room, the blistering
gold of chrysanthemums, we are never separate.

We resist: memory selects the same events,
the body selects the same responses.
Yesterday, the flock of grackles twisting
above the flat roofs of factories
formed the mathematical sign
for infinity, while, through the slate blue mass
of clouds at twilight, the last light bled.
The lamps in the valley tangled like jewels.
And always, the cool, unsettling questions.

Rain creates, admit it, a delicious tedium.
We resist: we hoard
between our legs the odor of turned earth.
For the self-conscious animal, awe,
like doubt, is a biological fact.
Admit it. Union
is by definition undistinguished.

Around here at night the ground dissolves, the houses lilt
on the still water. Like boats. Like cells.
The foghorns pulse whatever it is that gives
life through this house and the next. It filters
through brick and clapboard, strands of hair, slivers
of bamboo. It fills the avenues.

Under the gibbous moon, the city
like a ponderous sea mammal spumes, sinks and rises.
Inside us, heart and lungs float like insouciant fish in
flesh, in air. When we chafe out elbows, the cells
must whisper. *Who can bear to be forever listening?*

Like your voice in my ear, your hand
shielding my eyes, this rain must diminish
the senses of God, permit
intent, between breath and body, the voluntary
gasp, the merciless act of devotion.

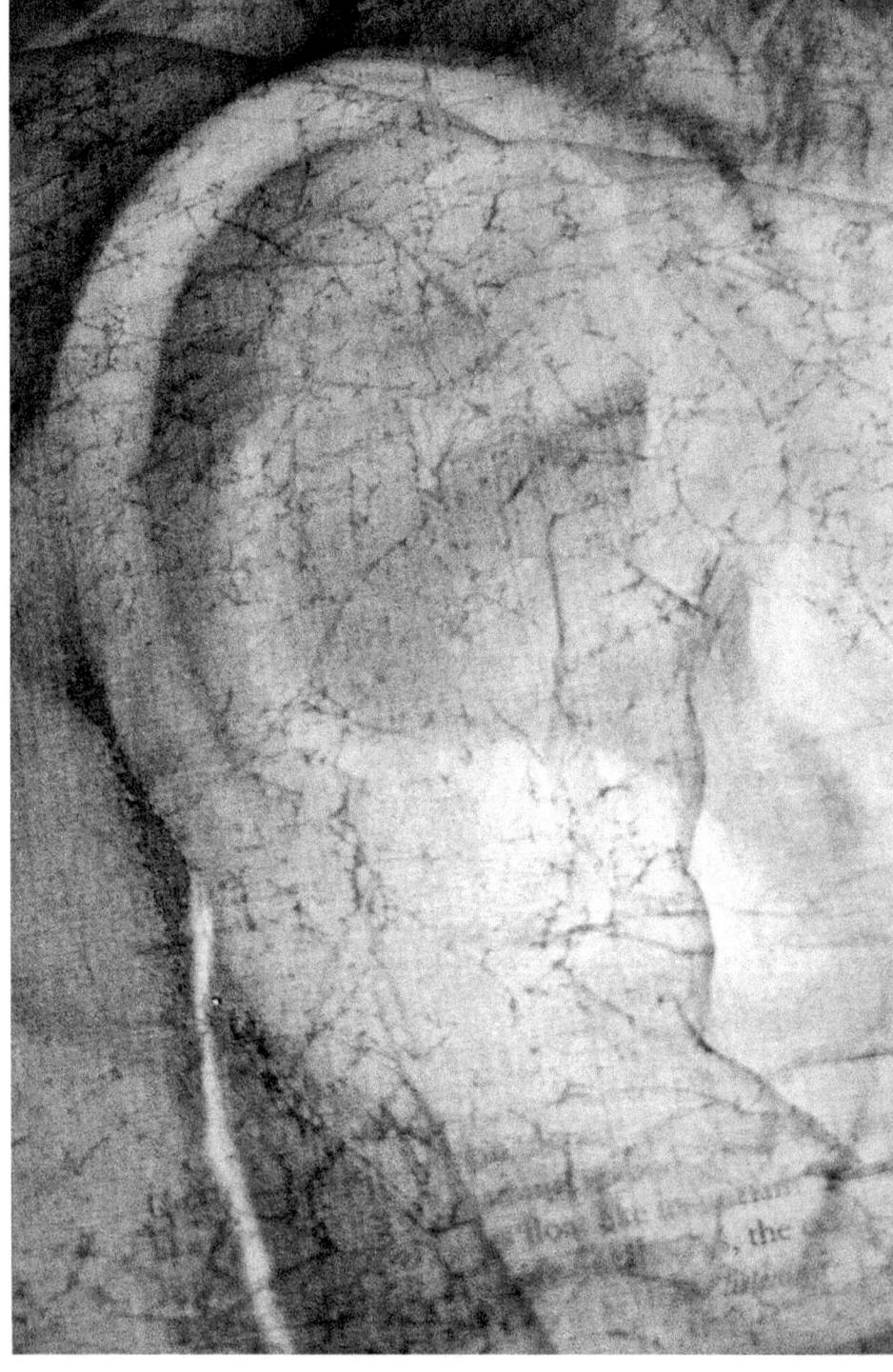

MARTINIQUE

i

Even at night, the horned cow grazes
on hibiscus and its own worn tether.
In the muddied lane, we stop, turn,
and turn again.

Soon we will be, won't we, tethered
like any domestic animal by habit,
goaded by a grumble from one
of our several stomachs. Hear it!

Even now, under the drone of the tree frogs—
how relentlessly she works that cud
of petals and leaves, hemp and leather.
Hear it!

No millstone can grind finer than those teeth,
no press squeeze more sugar from cane.
Lune de miel...bah!
The moon is pure stone. Pure!

If we wanted, could we stare her down?

ii

What was it you said?
With a thud the hearts of the tree frogs
catch in their belled brass throats
fall back into their belled brass bellies.
"This is something more—"
What was it you said?
The flamboyans shudder
animate as the drums.
We do not touch each other.
We do not touch ourselves.
Squalid animals leap from limb to limb
of the dead trees inside us.
This is something more primitive
then fear. *What was it you said?*

iii

Tonight the moon sloughs enough light
to make a path upon the water
from Anse Mitan to Fort de France.
Would we be making a mistake to take it?

The wind and the waves keep pace
with the shuddering flamboyans.
It's unspeakable. Neither of us
has found a moment of peace here—
but was that what we came for, what
we wanted? Habit
grinds the old phrase out
against the bowled mouth:
If this is…If this is…if.
And would we be making a mistake to take it?

Above us the moon caves in like a mortar.
The salt waves batter the bright curve of sand.
In the shadows, under the resonant trees,
shocked, you watch me pestle my own hard heart.

iv

Look!
Two white arms reach round the harbor,
clutching it like a honey pot.
The moon fawns upon its own
reflection. Morose as Pierrot,
it hoards the clotted dark.

v

I belong to no one. I give myself freely,
like so much dross. Poor man!
Penury is the possession of this breast
bruised gold by my own fist.
Look!

Will you take now, my love, paucity—
hibiscus and horned cow, squalid
drums and flamboyans, this
bitter, breathing sea?

vi

What was it you said?
Yes?

THEY KNOW

As water brimming holds
for a second in the air above
the glass the shape
of the glass—

they know—
these old Chinese women sitting in a row
on the opposite bench, bright
hands folded in their laps,
their eyes closed, their faces
slack—

on clear days the world
has a definite limit—
blue—
just beyond what we thought
the world could hold.

TERESA

Every morning, fearless, Teresa flings her life
over her shoulder, strides in broad daylight
down Judah Street to the ocean.
Only the slant of her back is defiant.
The wind teases the purple cloth
until it grazes her collar, the gathered edge
of the pillowcase, a taunt, a warning.

I named her for what I thought
her wanderlust. But Teresa hangs around.
When the fog and twilight erase houses,
street signs, even that willful purple turban,
Teresa stands steadfast in the catch basin.
She tosses her head back if you call out
in warning, fearful of the cars
that hiss and shriek from Twin Peaks to the ocean.

Teresa, I call her, for she finds faith
in the circumscribed, could continue,
like the saint, her silent devotions
anywhere, but best here under the jangle
of pots and pans, a life's worth
tumbled into a soiled blue pillowcase
and bound with a last majestic remnant
of that ravelled purple crown.

Warm, she says. I stand here because it's *warm*.

ped fighting anything but thorns and heat
ity so high it was like living inside a mouth.

parade. This is accurate
curate, and for a moment painles
hook scraping again and again

II
BRANDYWINE

BIRDNESTERS

The air is filled with feathers,
with the pulsations of wings. Hear it?
A man lifts a flaming torch in his left hand
and batters the sleeping birds from the trees.
He looks as if he were dancing, he reaches so high
with the light—and the club.
The second man, his back to the torch bearer,
raises a club in his right hand.
He wears a shock of straw tied to his back.
At his feet, an old woman kneels,
a red kerchief on her head, her arms outstretched
gathering the warm, feathered dead.
A young boy grips a bird in his hands so tightly
the wings stretch and the feathers spring apart like fingers.
It is a scene from Millet's childhood.
"And you have not seen it since you were a boy?"
someone asked him and he answered, "No,
but it all comes back to me as I work."

It comes: the heaving, feathered dark, the soft
thwap of the wooden clubs, the soft chest thrumming
inside the fist, those wings that close over
a boy's fingers soft as God's own hands.
It all comes back to him: the unbearable
tenderness of those gray tumbling wings,
how one wishes to kneel under them, fingers sprung
wider than feathers. It all comes back:
All those dazzled bodies falling into the light
man's made from pitch and twists of straw or bark,
the light that rises like a single blinding wing,
like a club, like an arm without a hand, a man
with nothing left to live for but himself.

It all comes back. The child's elation
at the ghastly dance, his pure hunger
for the flesh feathered by pitch and flame.
It all comes back to him now when his sight
fails him, his hand weakens, he is
what he beats from the pulsing air,
loose feathers, shivering
pillar of light, wing
of wood, a child's voluptuous
and thrumming greed
for the hot soft sweep of life.

...smiles back to him now
...m, his hand weakens,
...ts from the pulsi...
...thers, shivering,
...ight, wing...
...a child's voluptuou...
...d thrumming greed for th...

SPORTSMANSHIP

i

"Look. Can't you see anything?"
he asks me again and again.
He twists his head wildly,
as if my voice gave him pain.
Nothing. And then I see
his ear is a perfect rush
of blue under the thin, freckled skin.
He claps his hand over it
evading my touch.
"I give up. I'm not wrestling again."
"Don't," I say, truly shocked.
"Don't *stop.*"

ii

My son is two, crying himself blue
in the face. He stands alone
in the middle of the floor,
his fists clenched at his side,
his knees lifting and dropping
like a prisoner of war on a forced march.
No, no, no he wails. The other child,
a hand on his mother's shoulder,
looks puzzled. The mother leans forward,
a wooden block balanced on her open hand.
"Go on," she says. "Hit him. It's fair."
My son twists his head wildly
as if he didn't hear. His feet
keep plodding on the carpet

getting nowhere. "He won't," I say.
"He doesn't want to hurt anyone."
As I speak, my hands lock neatly
as tumbrils behind my back.
I know there is no comfort I can give him.
He's always been this way.
He wants to change the world.

iii

My son screams and pushes his friend
out from under the kitchen table.
"Give it back," he yells. "Give it back."
He is four, his friend, Chris, six.
My son reaches out with his left arm.
Chris waves his empty hands in the air.
He twists his head to hear his mother.
"Nothing, I don't have anything. I just said—"
"Please," my son cries. "Give it back to me."
"What?" I ask him. "My *hand*.
He cut off my *hand*."
"I was just pretending—"
"Give it back," I say.
"How?" Chris waves his hands in disgust.
My son lurches forward, grabs at the air.
He approaches me now with his left hand out,
flattened, as if he were balancing something.
I accept what he offers me. I can't see
for pity. I kneel beside him.
"Fix it," he whispers. "Hurry."

iv

"I want to walk by myself," he tells me.
"I don't want to wait for the bus.
I don't like the cold. I don't like the standing still."
"Your friend Hannah. Can't you wait with her?"
"I don't like her brother." I smile,
lean back on the stairs. He glares.
"He's crazy. You say something he doesn't like,
he puts his hands round your neck and chokes you."
"How old is he?" I lean forward.
"Ten. I come to his *elbow*.
Like you are to me here."
He leans over me on the stair
He puts his hands on my neck.
"Like *this*," he says. He presses down on my windpipe.
I shove him back. I can feel his breastbone giving
under my hand. It's automatic. All of it.
The blood leaping in my temple, the force.
"You too," he says, slipping down the wall.
He begins to cry. "You *too*," I say.
"That *is* what you did back, isn't it?"
"No," he says, holding his head with both hands.
"That just hurts him. It doesn't stop the stinging
in my throat." I hold him close.
I am wild with fear. How can he feel
he has a choice? The hand closes
over my own throat. I bury my face
in his shoulder. We are both lost.
We know it.

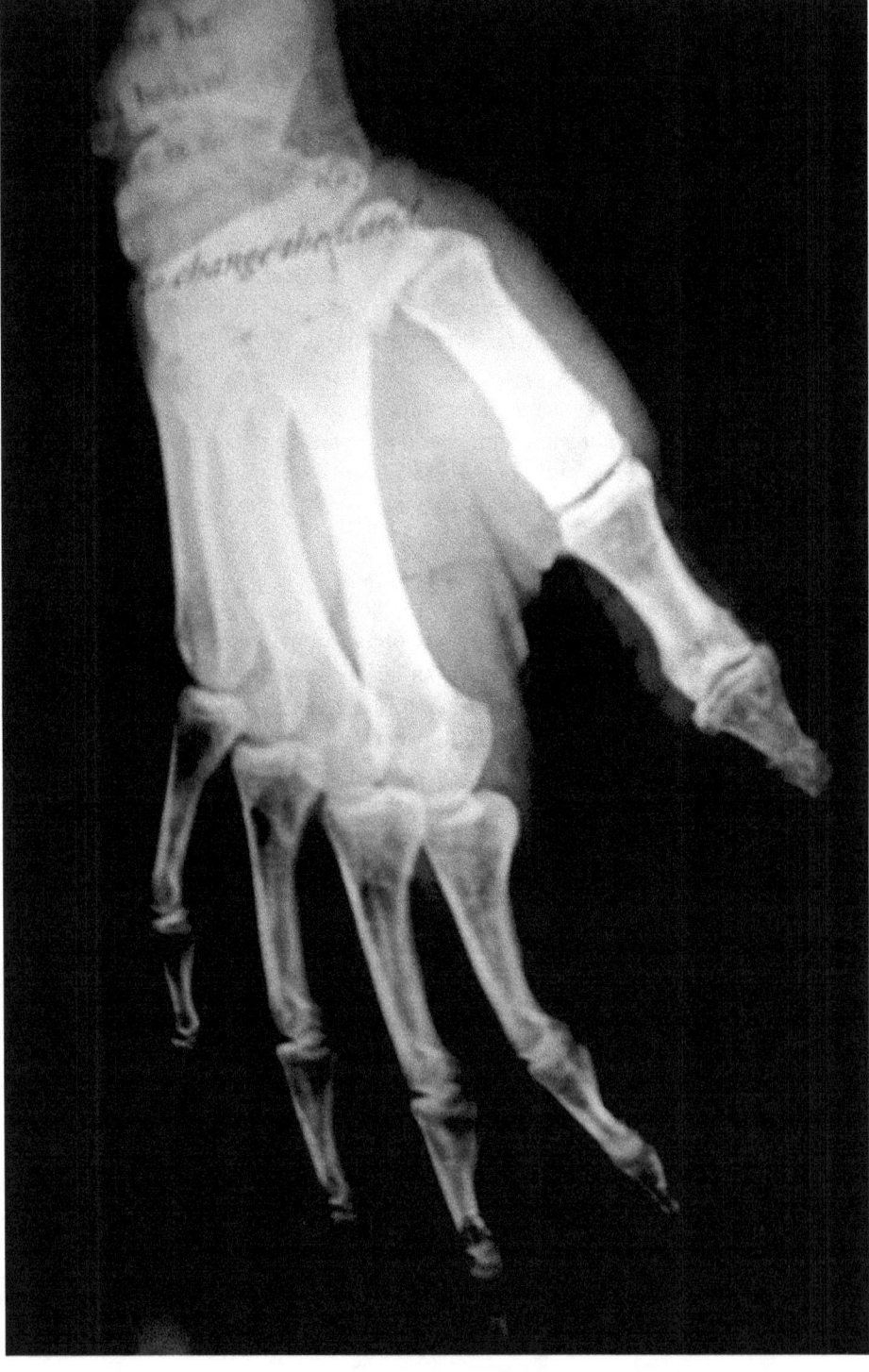

v

"I'm going to quit. I can't take it."
He looks at me, long face, narrowed eye.
Waiting. "How many times in your life are you—"
"Hundreds," he says triumphantly. "Maybe
thousands. What are you going to make of it?"
Tenderly he cups his hand around his ear, groans.
"Soon I'm going to look like a moron.
For what? He was ten pounds lighter.
He grabs on wherever he can. He won't let up."
My son sits down on the other chair. I think
at first he's smiling, but what distorts his face
is pity. "I cried. I went off and cried."
I look away. *No son of mine.*
"Where everyone could see?"
"What does it matter? He hurt me. He won.
That's what *I* want," he mutters. "Just once."
"You can't," I say. "You can't let them know
what you're feeling." The sky is blue.
His face is dark as the coming nightfall.
"What do you want of me?" He cups his ear
like my deaf grandmother.
I want to bury him in my arms.
Change, I yell. *I want you to change
yourself.*

SNOW WHITE ROSE

I am so alone this morning
with the two perfect roses chosen
by Anna and Sarah, white
and red, to console me.
I think of your net
of purity and silence.
I think of the two girls
at such cross purposes to each other
but equally perfect. I think of Anna's
obsession with white: talcum powder,
sugar, the insides of cookies,
crushed ice, her ballerina slip
that she strips to quicker than our mouths
can purse to tell her no.
I think of how she shames my prudish son
and angers her mother and how
this question she can't phrase
in any other way but action
still wakes her while her mother sleeps
and propels her to the kitchen
and the flour bin, or to the bath
and tin of talc. I think of the mother's voice
raised in anger because she is tired
and her daughter is undependable
and I think of the pure sorrow
of the child who loves her mother
but who also knows that white
is cold and sweet and silky,

that it is dangerous as teeth,
secure as a diaper, nothing
language can reach or master,
that she is, as she stands silently
memorizing the curve of her mother's white
eyelid, no different.

HEAVEN

My idea of heaven is light
playing across a white wall.
To think we live now in a house
eternity will never enter—
just because that woman,
suffering, a neighbor tells us,
from 'old-timer's disease,' twenty
years ago papered this duplex, cellar
to roof, with obsessive patterns
of the world's making.
There's no getting away from her
unless we want to lie on our backs
and stare at the ceiling—
at the blooming water stain
the plumber won't come and clean away
although I've called him every day for a month.
I've given up. This isn't an inch of our home
she hasn't left her stamp on—
African violets in the bathroom,
kalanchoes and swiss ivy in the kitchen, gold
fleur de lis in one bedroom, silver
fleur de lis in the other, green
daisies smaller than a baby's fingernail
all over the study, yellow and white
piping in the halls and all the living room.
Some days it makes me want to die
or go crazy. It can't be ignored—
not the frenzied courage or the bad taste
or the decay. A hand placed carelessly
makes the paper blister like skin.

When brushed by a sleeve or a skirt,
it shreds like a woman's heartbroken voice.
But it's this yellow that defies me completely.
It swallows light, dulls
the color of anything set against it.
It is pale, but insistent
as the idea of her body resting
in the high, barred hospital bed,
the mind dissolving into velvet, mold.
Soon there will be nothing but this piss
yellow paper to remind us that we too
may one day ask the plumber to play
duets with us, or shrill like birds
in the holly bush as we try, dead
of night, blind as bats,
to tear the rat's nest from our brassy hair.

Perhaps I was wrong all along, thinking
that, like light on mineral white
paint or scumbled plaster, heaven was,
by definition, everything except us?
Certainly not jaundice, yellow teeth,
bed sores, spongy bones, a mind
playing Chopin mazurkas in double time,
the gnarled fingers stammering and the tongue
slowly touching the root and roof of the mouth
as the lips grimace and purse over a single word—
loneliness—and the young plumber blinks
at the skin buckling free of the muscle
and fat in an old woman's breast,

disgusted and afraid and suddenly mad
enough to gather with his bare hands
the light that shattered harmlessly
around his wife's bare hip, the matted
sheet, and her lover's grasping fist,
that covered the bathroom floor
when he was seven and his mother's rose
glittering like crystal from her morning bath
into his father's brawny arms—

                To think we've chosen
to live like this—in rooms stained with semen
and tear and steeping water, with the sweet
consolations of Brahms, and the mad ricochet
of Chopin's mazurkas forever reminding us
this is the promise of heaven, this
indiscriminate light licking
our indiscriminate flesh until
our faces purse and grimace,
the tongue tests the roof and root
of our mouths, the one word
reverberates through every cell
as if through crystal, and we turn
in true and terrible yearning
against each other.

reverberates through every cell
as if through crystal, and we turn
in true and terrible yearning
against each other.

IL N'EST PIRE AVEUGLE QUE CELUI QUI NE VEUT PAS VOIR

I share the proverb with you
as we are crossing the street to the museum.
You like it. I hate the very idea
of blindness. I think it is the equality
of the terms that appeals to you.
Il n'est pire—It is no worse.
I don't believe it for a minute.
In the museum, we separate. Today, you say,
I will concentrate on the present.
I mount the stairs, you disappear
down the nearest corridor. Light,
it's all I can think about. The torches
of Millet's peasants dazzling the dozing flock.
Turner's water and sky resonant with flame.
A woman stands before *The Burning of the Houses
of Parliament* taking notes. She is trying to train
her eye, curb her impatient fingers, just as I am.
I blink, turn my head. It's lost, all lost,
the bridge, the flaming buildings, flaring Thames.
It's true: most of us can't look at a painting
any longer than it takes to peel an orange.

I retrace my way down the great stairs,
follow the corridor you've chosen. It's not you
I'm seeking, but Matisse's odalisques, Duchamp's nudes.
Today I discover a sculpture by Brancusi:
Statue for the Blind. It is sealed in a glass box.
Even in the mind's cave, it is a white shape.
I imagine taking a man's hand—not yours—

and placing it beneath mine on the marble.
I imagine seeing as he does, as the blind do, *willingly*,
through the tips of their fingers, through their resonant
skin, a shape that is endless, mammoth, good,
cool as the hand that cups my breast,
smooth as the voice that says, *Te amo, Te amo.*

We meet at the appointed time. Smile.
I would not dream of telling you where I've been.
You would not dream of asking. *Il n'est pire*
…fire…*il n'est pire*…snow.
Il n'est pire…liar…*il n'est pire*…love.

BRANDYWINE

The gold field spreads out from the river
like a dusty wing. The air is dry and hot.
It could be August—but it's March.
We are out walking, the whole family, single file
along paths that were impassable
when we first came here late last July.
Then, the river banks were covered with vines,
thistles, briars, such a weight of green
we all stopped fighting anything but thorns and heat
and humidity so high it was like living inside a mouth.
Today we all walk silently. It's as if we've reached a clearing
inside ourselves where there is exactly
what stretches out before us: to the right, a field gold
with dead grasses, to the left a wide, slow-moving river.
Around our feet, red-winged beetles flutter up,
drift to rest on the bent grasses, the few new leaves.
We round a bend in the river and see two canoes
drifting sideways to the current. Nosing close
to the bank, they buffet each other. They are both
filled with men. There is loud talk, laughter, among them.
They are probably drunk. They are all young.
"What's happening?" they ask me. They assume
we are alone, my son and I. Even when you pass them,
five minutes later, I'm not sure they will connect us,
we seem so separate. This is accurate
as the day is accurate, and for a moment painless
as an unbaited hook scraping again and again
the river's quivering flank.

Tching! The water dripping from the eaves. Tching! The branch brushing the water's edge. Tching! The bird shivering with song. We were meant to be this way. Secret, quiescent, open, tching! *Open*

ENTRE L'ARBRE ET L'ÉCORCE IL NE FAUT PAS METTRE LE DOIGT

Tch, tch, tching! A song like cracking seeds.
The crows groan in the bare branches. Unh! Unh!
A squirrel scuttles through dry leaves.
In the sky, one long white feathered plume.

A hawk, turning in circles, disappears, glints
back, swoops darkly round, disappears into mist
and flashes back again, bright sliver
of steel, torn metal.

There is a woman here who lost a child last year.
Quietly, she paints, and paints, and paints.
She keeps herself to herself, but when you speak
to her she smiles. She gives directions
to this lake.

The boat house, she has told me, look out
at the lake from there. *Look out.*
Nothing could stop me from stepping into that dark,
damp, reverberant enclosure. *Look out.*
Weeping, tching! tching!

I pause halfway across the slanted floor.
The water drips from the eaves
onto the concrete quais, onto the still brown water.
She knew, did she, what I would find here?
I never want to leave.

Tching! The water dripping from the eaves. Tching!
The branch brushing the water's edge. Tching!
The bird shivering with song. We were meant
to be this way. Secret, quiescent,
open, tching! *Open*

in the dead for
Like stones. Like di
on da.
sink like sto
said, down.

III
WOMAN DEVOURED BY FISHES

TO WELCOME ME, YOU PAINT
THE WALLS WHITE

You erase your life. The bleached squares
left by pictures that hung there for years.
In the same spirit I draw all the nails
you've driven into plaster over the last decade
and save them, torqued and rusted and promising something
I can taste on the back of my tongue. When that's done,
I open the box I brought with me
and draw out blank, gray paper the same lost
color as the walls, uncap my pen, and wait—
soon shadows begin to stir under the new,
runneled paint. A hand print appears.
Under its weight, the shadows of the yellow mums
and purple statis hold stone still, like a startled animal.
This is just as wrong and just as right
as the vows we are making: *Forever. Life.*

Last night under the streetlight
you told me you couldn't see yourself
living this way forever. So many lies
and so many revelations, and nothing—
nothing changes.

SOTANO

Against a gray discus, the figure wavers,
flailing the light like a swimmer.
I can't tell if he's coming or going.
Last night under the streetlight
you told me you couldn't see yourself
living this way forever. So many lies
and so many revelations, and nothing—
nothing changes.

We've all been undermined.
Today I have a bruise on my neck, as if the night
air had slipped under my skin. Come here,
you said to me. Come here. Dragging
the blood from my veins—
as if it wouldn't have come willingly.
Come here, you said, and I felt my body looming
in the dark room, and I knew you would never find me,
even there, within your arms.

Desierto de Leones.
The pines tower, irreducibly green,
on the stony peaks and in the deep valleys.
The desert, the monks knew, is within.
Lions pad across the parched veldt half a world away.
We act as if we've come here to stay.

Even at arm's length, the candle dazzles.
A man wades out of shadow.
Passing, he shakes the air, and we feel

the true depth of the dark, how it hews into the stone
walls, bells the ceiling, pocks the earthen floor.
I never learn. So many lies and so many revelations
and nothing—nothing changes. Left alone with you
another ten minutes, again I would be lulled into happiness.

But already we have turned right and stand,
blinking, on the parched grass. "*Viejo*,"
a big brute of a man shadows the blind vendor.
"I'll give you only a hundred for those candles."
The old man crosses his hands in his lap.

The vendor's wife shifts her buttocks.
Her hands too are crossed patiently over her pubis.
The light flickers over her face like a feather.
What's the difference, she thinks. Why not give them to him?

Tending the tentative flame, each hand grows mammoth.
The palm cups a void deeper than any sotano.
Desierto de Leones.
Behind us someone sees the light clasp
our heads, soft as flesh. *What's the difference?*

Now, held out against the sky, our candle
is a meager blue. We too could sell it—
or pass it, as we do, restlessly from one to another.
So much more than we had bargained for—
and never, the monks knew, enough.

LEVIN AT FOURTEEN

On his windowsill, I find pyres of burnt matches.
All this vacation, he's tried to case narcissus
and vivid bougainvillea in wax.
It's everywhere—a child's terrible
tenderness for the perishing world.
What a mess. Paraffin and soot,
scorched tins and a clotted brush.
I'll clean it up. He defends himself
with a man's voice, a novelist's eye.
My Anna, he sighs as the lights go out.
Sit beside me. I could be Levin, but I'm not married.
Tell me, could you, how the story ends?
I'll write another, I assure him, with no train.
Or Vronsky, he says, burying his head in his pillow.
My migraines, he murmurs, are only a way of stretching
my brain to let everything in. No light,
he says. *No light.*

Days ago, he fashioned a brooch
from an orange lily, wax, a borrowed safety pin
for a beautiful woman named Milagros.
When he found the baby in the *Rosca de Reyes*
you gave us, he picked up a knife. I hate,
he said, all the babies in the world.
And then he ate. And ate.
He wants, today, to be a Buddhist monk
fattened on the sweetest wisdom.
What's to keep him, he asks me
as he raises his face full to the sun,
from leaving you again?

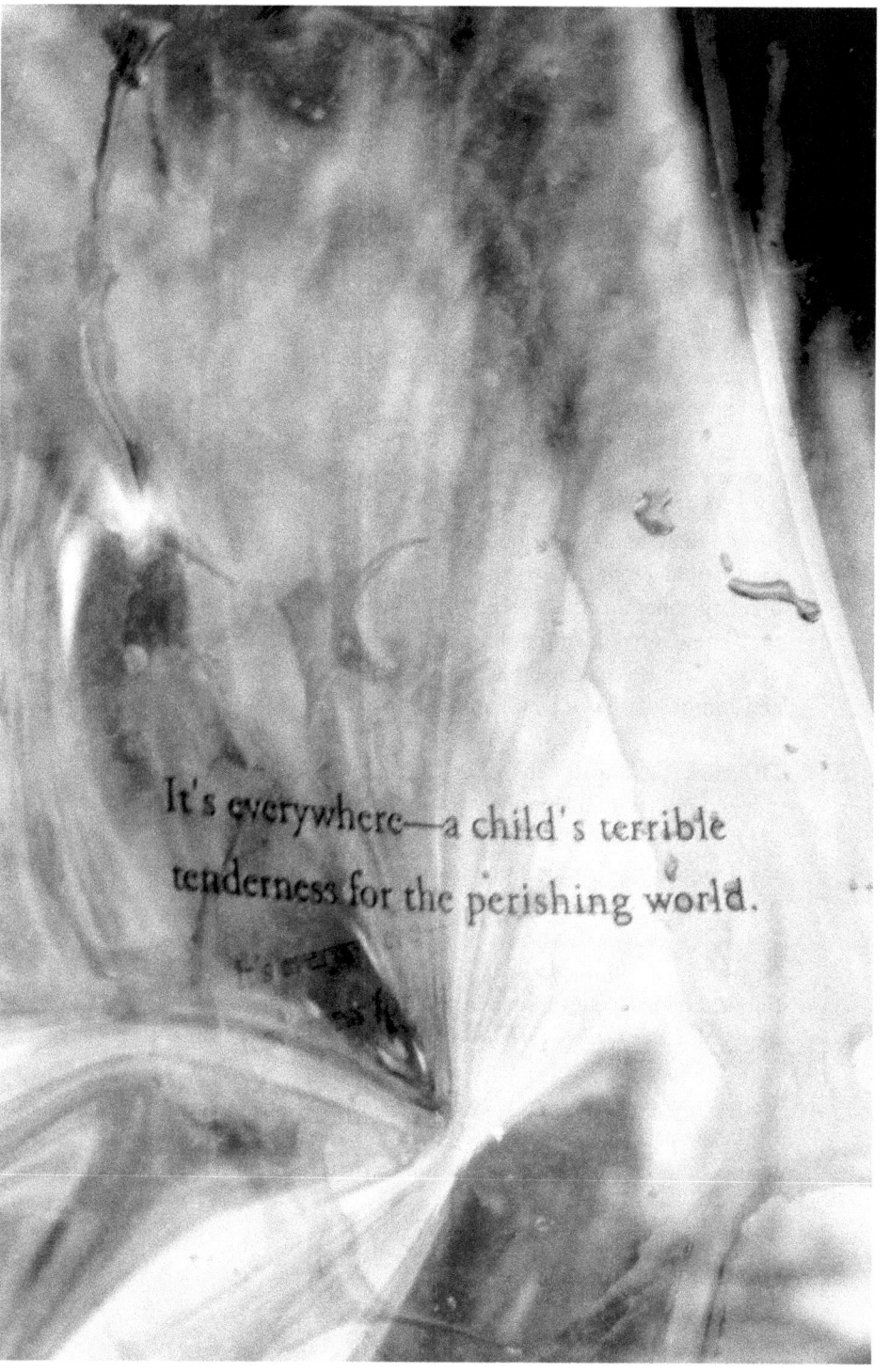

WOMAN DEVOURED BY FISHES

i

In the discreet ones, the dogs only sniff
at the *mons* and buttocks of women,
in the worst ones they've turned them
on their heads and are devouring them
there, where they are most tender.

An old man cradles his prick while he watches two
toads copulate. Small fishes tear away the belly
of a large one, until they expose the human, female thighs
they knew it had been masking all along. In the mouth
of the mask rides a small naked woman. I don't know—
and I know—what it all means.

Delicately, an alligator snares a woman's skirt on its teeth,
a naked man with alligator scales, spread wings, erect
sex nods to his *semblable*, the serpent, the piranha,
the dog, the toad. What fine lines
distinguish us.

These are *dibujos*, drawings,
published in the cultural pages of the Sunday paper, work
of a major artist, *more furious than Picasso*, writes a famous
anthropologist in their defense. *Nowhere do you see a purer
rendition of the evil of sex.* It's a ten page spread.
I fold the paper, embarrassed by the stares of the other passengers.
It's not fair. I bought it not to look like such a stranger here.

ii

I don't walk like the woman here.
I walk faster and in flat shoes and as if no one were watching.
I walk as if I were fighting the forces that bind us
to the earth. I walk this way by the men hissing
like snakes as they stumble out of the pulque bar,
by the adolescent boys sitting on the hoods of their cars,
by the blind led bandaged from the eye hospital, the smiling curate
hurrying to the church. I walk this way through the park,
by the lovers on benches, the children on swings,
then I stop. To my left, a light wind lifts
a row of tall yellow lilies higher into the light
and something in me lifts and steadies. *I am happy,*
I think. *At this minute I am perfectly happy.*
And then I turn and see first the brown belly,
the pants snagged at his knees, the brown hands cradling
the limp penis. I think *I should warn him.*
I think, *My look is meant to be some kind of absolution.*

And then I turn my head and I walk past him, fast,
as I would the breathless curate hurrying to the church.
Another man going into the toolshed watches me curiously,
as if he knew what had been sitting in wait for me back there,
and now, along with pity, I feel fear. Maybe it isn't absolution
they're after…I don't know anymore
than I know what breaks the thin skin of sleep every night
and tears all peace from me: the voice,
so childish and wild, saying, *If you don't say I am perfectly right,*

saying, *Don't you love my penis*, saying, *Admit you want this*,
saying, *When can I do whatever I want with you? Mordidas*,
all of them, my flesh the price.

                      I don't know what holds me—
on a garden path or in a bed. I know it isn't desire. It hurts.
All this hurts. Like the teeth of crocodiles, piranhas, dogs.
The pain of it makes me want to kill myself to stop it…
like the woman modeling for the famous painter, when she saw
the fishes nosing open mouthed against her thighs
that he had called once *beautiful*, when at last she understood
the meaning these words held for him—*belleza, deseo*—
and then he turned to her, smiling, wanting her
to love him for it.

EL DÍA DE LOS MUERTOS

A metro car is no metaphor for life.
One day, between stops, an old woman wanted to get off
and her daughter wouldn't let her. *Indios*.
The mother's face was pocked, her gray hair frayed
from her braids. Maybe she was drunk.
She was weaving and her daughter gripped her
by the wrist when the car doors opened.
She yelled and tried to free herself.
She looked around for help.

The teenage girls chewed gum and adjusted each other's earrings.
The businessman eyed the loudspeakers. The daughter had her
head down and her arm out, her hand clamped over her mother's
wrist. When the doors closed, her mother stopped shouting
and started slapping her with the flat of her hand
as if she were a small child. Her long hair rippled with the blows.
As if she were a figure of her imagination, her mother
beat her; her mother beat her as if she were real.

The color of the daughter's face never rose,
and she never looked around, and she never let go.
Did she hate the people who saw the shape of her suffering
and did nothing? Her mother reeled in her grip.
Another passenger steadied her. Again the mother's hands closed
around the daughter's head like a bell around a clapper.
When their stop came, the daughter stood and led her mother
tenderly out of the car. Her bag was filled with *cebollas*
and *papas*, *chiles*, and *elote*.

Does she know cockscomb is a dream of vengeance that can unfold
on any mother's grave, and marigolds are more bitter
and clean than understanding? Tonight, preparing dinner
for my son, I imagine her in her own kitchen, how carefully
she draws the spines from the *nopal*, cuts the corn from its ear,
how the food will turn at her touch into hunger
and thirst and her mother will weeping eat of it
and drink of it and then in her agony will begin beating
her daughter's black hair, the hard bones of her skull
as if they were nothing but clay, something that could be worked
into perfect love and obedience, and the daughter will never
lift her head or her hand to stop her, but only draw her closer
by the pressure of her fingers on that flesh that opens itself
to pains as easily, just as easily, as her own,
or the Saviour's, or the small boy who drew,
dripping, from his pail this morning, cockscomb and marigold,
all the children screaming, *¡Dinero! Dinero por mi calavera.*
Money! Money for my skull.

We *are* the sum of history: *Dios de los muertos.*

We are the new beginning.

LA ONDA

¿Qué onda? Around here it means, "What's happening?"
"What's going down?" Mystic initiation, a man tells you,
the first step, where you let go of everything you know,
is like a wave. *If you fight it you drown.*

¿Qué onda? If you fight it, you drown.
You keep repeating this as the room lifts in the moonlight,
when you can't tell the difference between the walls or the curtains
or the light on your skin or the wide white waste your life can seem.
When you don't know where love lies, or death,
when you don't know what has you in its grip. *¿Qué onda?*

If you don't move, the anguish will. *Qué onda.*
If you fight, it's the same thing. *Qué onda.*
If you scream no one would understand a word you're saying.
It would mean no more than the crazy rooster
marking off the hours of the night. *Qué onda. Qué onda.*

So, because you want to live, you just ride it, *qué onda,*
like moonlight, foam. You know it is all down there,
the mother drunk and alone, the father who watches
his infant son running through cars and doesn't raise a hand
to stop him, and the one who strokes his daughter
to a dreadful silence, the husband, his face puffed
with pain, *you have done such harm,*
and your sister driving the empty swing bright as a blade up
into your own face, the man forcing you
to go down, go down—

If you fight it, you join the dead for sure.
They are pure. Like stones. Like dirt. And they know
one thing for certain. *Qué onda.*
Swallow it whole, we'll sink like stones.
We'll go, like the man said, down. *Go down*

I HAVE STUMBLED ON SOMETHING

Church doors askew against the sun-daubed wall,
steeple listing into the clean May sky, it's too late
for morning mass. They've crowded unbidden to the left
of the aisle. A woman turns from the altar cradling white
gladiolas against her worn apron. She hands them off,
stalk by stalk, holding back one for herself.
Then an old woman bends and grips the hand of a small boy,
and it is like some living thing,
this rippling progression through the pews. Everyone bows
to the Virgin and leaves their white flower
on the table set outside the communion rail.
I keep wondering when the priest will come
to put a stop to it.

Again they take what they're given, white glads,
again the old woman cries out, again they follow her
like sheep, like sweet believers, weaving through the pews,
a single beast. They could do this forever.
Giving. Receiving.
Indian givers.
They are all Indian givers.

I turn away, my eyes burning.
What I would give never to have seen this.
I would give flowers. I would give words.
I would give a lock of my son's hair.
A shot of my mother's gin. Colostrum.
And I would give the very same things—

flowers and words and all the love and the hurt
of half a lifetime to sit here, just one
among them, listening to that voice
so sure and worn, like a pestle
working in the mortar after all the seed is gone.

...that I would like never to...
...e flowers. I would...
...e a lock of my son'...
...r mother's gin. Co...
...give the very same...
...ords and all the lo...
...me to sit here, just...
...listening to that voi...
...orn, like a pestle...
...mortar after all...

THIS IS THE FLOWER

i

This is the flower you keep giving the Virgin
and keep taking back as the liar does his trust
in the listener, who needs to believe for two.
It's not enough to keep your mouth shut,
not to move. It's faith the liar asks for, blind
trust, and if he sees it flicker and die in your eyes,
you might as well be damned. It's not a question of love.
This is the flower you give to the Virgin, still and bright
as a child's eye at night when the light hits:
faith, boundless faith.

ii

Your father's hand strokes you into silence.
You are a good girl, like your mother, like his lover,
and you won't betray him. It is like fire, his touch,
but you don't cry out. Who would listen?
Who would understand?
Joan of Arc? The flames sang in her ears like angels.
Sacajawea? The men trusted her like little children.
Jane Addams? For her the cries of the poor
were as comforting as the sounds of her father's saw mill,
working, forever working, for the good...

You will not betray him. He is afraid.
That is what makes the fire in his touch.
This isn't love. His voice is soft.
He doesn't want to wake your sister. This is just
between you. *This is just.*

He stares into your eyes. You have seen
nothing. You know nothing. He looks at you
with the cruel need of the liar. *You must believe for two.*
And you do. You know nothing. You have seen nothing.
You will never betray him. He is a good man. He is
your father. He is power. He is love. *He is a liar.*

His touch is like a single wave of flame and his voice
is like the wind fanning the heat and the light
through thousands of trees, the whole world is blazing,
it is like heaven when God is chiding the cherubim. I believe,
you think. I believe I will die if he leaves me
alone in the dark with the smell of ashes and my own piss
and this loneliness that is so deep it must be sin.

He searches your face again and again. There is nothing there
but what he wishes to see: Love. Trust. Obedience.
You are good, he says. The words are like flames.
The good don't suffer like this, only the wicked.
Little flower, he pleads, *trust me*.

You make your mind quite blank, like a mirror.
You will do anything so he won't leave you alone
with her and her fury or the loneliness
that is so deep it must be sin, somewhere even God
can't hurt you.

IF THE IMAGE OF THE DIVINE IN US IS OUR DESIRE

for communion, if time is the distance
between desire and satisfaction, the lust
of the mystic is no greater than that of the exile,
the peasant, the mother for her dead child.
It's nothing like the chiming clock of pesos
that measures the play of these children
in their bright ribbons and starched dresses,
or the hunger of the woman I saw just days ago
on the metro who swept the floor with her white poncho
she was so bent. Her red hair fell
over her eyes as she reached out for change
or a silver pole or the shoulder of a seated passenger
and we all knew she was going to fall, walking
over her own poncho as if it were a carpet,
and all this time one terrible vowel that might be love
or its denial swelled through her toothless mouth.

    Silently, a man, then a woman, a young girl peeled
her hand from their chests, their necks, their faces
and placed it on the pole, but she wouldn't stay still,
she kept reaching out for more and stumbling over
her own clothes while this one sound
like some man's dream of ecstasy
threatened to swallow us. Whole.

    Never had I imagined the patience of this *gente*,
how no one drew away from her touch, no one opened their mouth
to scold her, no one doubted, as I did, her blindness,

and no one cared. They peeled her hand off like wet cloth.
One life among millions, one convolvulus
on the red cockscomb. Empty.

    Her hand was empty and through her gums, clean
as a baby's, the music kept pouring and I imagined
time for her, anything to break the continuum of her song,
how it must be the sound of two coins chiming, the vertigo
of a train braking or speeding up, and the touch
of hands that smell of raw meat or fresh bread, excrement
or marigold, that take her own without *rechazo*
and put them elsewhere. I sat there waiting for her
to touch me, afraid that I might scream—
or silence us both with a kiss.

           of the exile,
      for her dead child
    running clock of pesos
   play of these children
       and starched dresses,
       the woman I saw just days ago on the metro
         with her white poncho
         Her red hair fell
           reached out for change
           shoulder of a seated passenger
              going to fall, walking
              as if it were a carpet,
              possible vowel that might be love
              through her toothless mouth.

    Silently, a man, then a woman, a young girl peeled
her hand from her chests, their necks, their faces
and placed it on the pole but she wouldn't stay still,
she kept reaching out for more and stumbling over
her own clothes, while this one sound
like some man's sound of ecstasy
threatened to swallow us whole.

       Never had I imagined the patience of this *gente*,
how no one drew away from her touch, no one opened their mouth
to scold her, no one doubted, as I did, her kindness,
and *no one cared*. They peeled her hand off like wet cloth,
one life among millions, one convolvus
the red cockscomb. Empty.

...eleton with the...
...m own feet
...ese pictures plead
... story.
...them is this: Still Life: 40.

...hole body aches when it sees
...ped photograph, black against an expanse
...f grass, the silhouette of a young boy.
...n a stand of rhododendron, he waits
...paralised, one drawn back close to his mouth.
...e could be swept away in a rage Of tenderness.

...ly responding to an idea, motherhood,
...n back m... violently... the nervous system
...ed him

BOOK III: 1990-1999
I
REIFICATION

CICATRICES

Some days the whole world speaks.
The snow cupped in the dark, arched hip,
the dreadful scars scoring the thighs,
the shy dry cleft between them, as if,
with a little will, the universe could be sealed
up again. Today, among the graves, I train my camera.
Even at this distance, my tongue can taste the whiteness
of the snow. My eyes touch the scarred bark and for a moment I can feel
the crazy glee of the suicide carving out a little breathing room.
That's it. Nothing destructive, just— These cicatrices never bled
although each spring they weep sweet sap from these tracks
made decades ago by some young kid's first thoughtless twists
of a pocketknife.

My hand enters the camera frame. I can't explain
what it feels like, the divorce and the connection—
Scars testify until the day we die. I. Thou.
In. Out. Used. We are all used.
I believe if I do not move I can't be accused.
It is not a question of will. Or guilt.
Transgression is something else entirely.

...on his sleeve as if to pat...
...thing humane. But with my...
Too close. Half a decade of... tears...
down my cheeks. I wanted to say something...
about forgiveness.

JARS

1

The color is untrue. The glass blue as a scoured sky,
the cloth soft as the skin of newly culled olives.
The real cloth is garish, ochre, and the glass clear,
but the photograph assures me, with its dazzle of shadow,
the tonal integrity of the glass and the cloth,
that concentration tempers us,
anneals what at first appears irreconcilable or just
harsher than the eye can tolerate.
My life before. My life after.
What separates them is nothing
but breath and a million synapses
that don't fire anymore. A quieter world.
More beautiful. Mysteriously
bereft. The objects of my meditation
never existed, are nothing but chance
excitations. I recognize this in the same second
I recognize pleasure in its purest rush,
something deeper, more generous than lust,
but not unlike, dangerously, in fact, akin.
All my life I have been sure there is another world
inside the page, outside the glass, whose air is warmer
and more enveloping, the simple taste
and touch of which will save me.
Nothing like the dense red must that covers the retina
when I am resting deep within the spirit,
where in a landscape littered, like a highway in Iraq,
with scorched cars and trucks, scoured
by whirlwinds of sand and ash, a mother,
clutching her child to her chest, kneels
before an angel made of spare body parts.

2

The jar and the shadows it casts
tell irreconcilable stories.

A friend draws hundreds of triptychs
recounting the assault of the psyche:
The tumbling stones of Samson's temple,
the archangel Gabriel's whole weight shifting toward
his admonishing left arm, the figure clinging
to the rim of the funnel that is the seventh circle
of hell— Years later in the quiet that presages waking,
I see at last how perfectly composed they have always been,
these endless circles of mythic destruction,
as if at the deepest level he always knew
there was a shape that could contain it—
all that anguish that felt so blind
and damaging, a caterwauling of souls
so primitive it still resonates
with the slightest graze of a man's skin.
And then I know, the way the sleeper waking in the dark knows,
before thought, before scent—
the hairs on his skin rising in warning—
something animate and untoward has approached.
Too close. Half a decade later, the tears course
down my cheeks. I wanted to say something
about forgiveness.

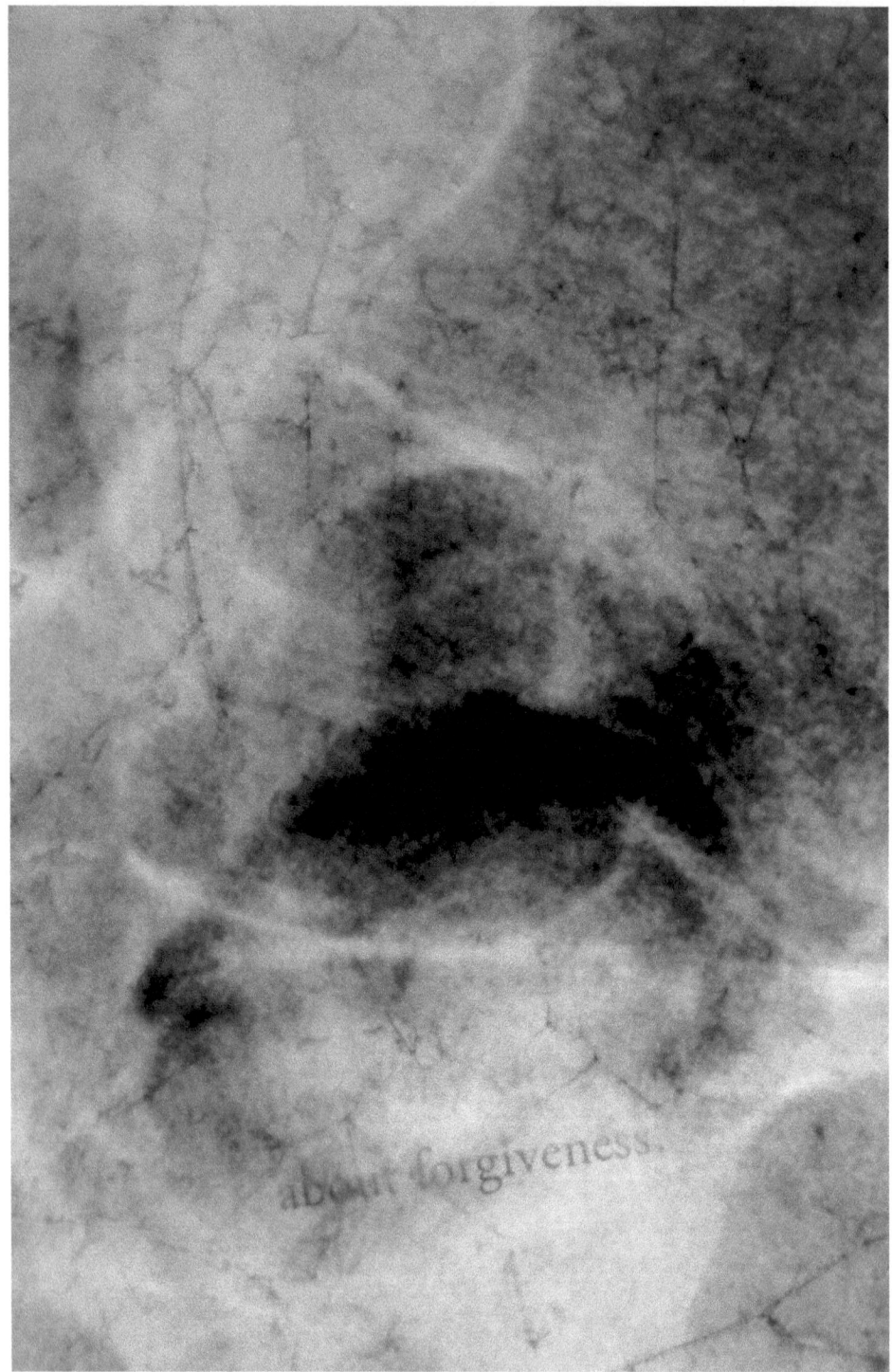

CRYPTIC

1

The eye sees some purely physical fit
between the stiff white packing used for Christmas gifts
and several strange totems collected, one thought,
par hasard, and having seen this, can't rest
until the four white caves are aligned, glued
and fitted with their counterparts. All art builds
like this, equal parts chance and will
and the delicate interleavings of small bones,
folds of molten glass, stones knotted tight inside
mangrove roots, and then, if we're lucky, something spills
free or, worse, heaves and subsides
just beneath the conscious mind.

2

There is a recurrent dream I have these days
whose dominant tone is consciousness. Under the flat
blue-hued fluorescent light in the ladies room
at my office, totally unembarrassed, thorough,
I extract from my tongue long gray worms.
Women enter and leave. Disease is nothing
to be ashamed of, just something to cure
I inform them by the swift sureness of my hand and arm.

I am not afraid. That is what startles me
when I wake and I wish there were someone
to whom I could explain, someone who will not respond
to the strangeness but the calm. A feeling quite unlike
the one I have looking at this tidy set of white crypts
I had hoped to use to set the past to rest.

3

One arched white space holds a red carnation,
a fine white skeleton spans the portal of the next,
the third closes tight as a fist around a gnarl
of seaworn rock and stone, while the last
harbors a figure of molten glass and ash
gathered from the rubble of a burned out house.
Some evenings, contemplating these, the bruising
red of the carnation, the way the glue has eaten
deep into one of the cavities, I sense something moving,
huge and startling, just under the surface of consciousness
and I feel completely unmoored—as if my days and my dreams
are equally deceiving.

4

I don't understand why the construction I've made
to harbor circumstance fills me with such sorrow,
as if, without knowing it, I have willed away tomorrow.
I keep thinking if I could put a name and a date,
an act—even rape—to what caved in my will
and selfhood, I would begin to heal.
I am lying now. *I believe if I forgive us all
I can lock the pain off.* Look at what I've built
to prove it: These smooth white caves give out,
like the uterus, only on the world.
There is no deeper retreat than this.
There is no deeper hurt.
See how I've separated them off, and bound them
together too, like years, or the stories we weave
to prove there is some necessary match, like cock
and cunt, between act and consequence.

On what terms do we live if we don't?

SPELLBOUND

A fence of nails weaves between rocks and small metal stars
and transistors that look as if they could stand in for humans.
A frail skeleton, elegant as a dressmaker's dummy, leans, illumined,
against the window pane, slightly out of scale—
and exactly right. Summer congeries arranged on a pantry sill.
The easy symmetry delights me each time I pass, as if beauty could be
captured that way, reaped from the beach with a haphazard
sweep of the hand. *L'art brut.*

In the small residues of light the year has left to us,
I reassemble these objects on a white cloth.
For balance, I close the fence and the light throws the shadows
of the nails in and out of the bright core like a braid of thorns.
Shored, the skeleton rests on the nail heads, opaquely white.
The austere photographs I make delight my artist son
because of their composition. They scare me.
It's something about the high contrast, he assures me. But it's not.
I'm not sure anymore what I want to wall in—or out.
I'm not sure it's under my control—any more than my own skin.
Touch me and the nerve ends flare like a wreath of flames.
But these photographs augur something worse. I can see how it folds back
into the shadow, perfectly inviolable, like the self
constrained to the brain pan. I do not believe God
intended us to live so closed away from one another,
I whisper at the altar rail and a priest wreathes my head
with her cool hands and whispers the prayer I never dared:
Feed her darkness.

REIFICATION

1

Let's take the skeleton plucked from tidewrack
early one morning in Truro. Let's go back even further
to the moment I paused amid searose and scrub
high on the bluff and heard as if it were the only sound
left on this whole earth, the clammer's rake
breaking through the still waters of the bay
and thought, this must be someone's idea of God.

What is the name for the way some days one's whole skin reverberates
until even one's bones thrill with the pressure
of the air displaced by what is purely other—some act
as simple as this: A rake forever breaking the integrity of the sea.

2

Let's take a shape like that of the skeleton
plucked from tidewrack one still morning in Truro
that leans, lucent, against my cold window pane.
Does it matter I don't care to reconstruct its species
because its contours are now so purely human, speaking
like an undraped dressmaker's dummy does
of all that the flesh can promise us.

Thinking to deliver myself into its power,
I've tried to capture its allure in photographs.
I've mounted them all on my bedroom wall
because they scare me unbearably. The bones seem
so opaque and dangerous tucked into the labial folds
of a bright white cloth, and I realize
that I, who have given birth to a child,
am giving birth now to bones, crushed snakes, scarred
bark and small palm crosses and cannot see
how this could possibly be a vision of freedom.

And still the bone speaks to me when I set it
again against the dusty pane and its hollows,
so like a woman's breasts and hips,
fill with light and I imagine there might be
some change as elemental as this that could take place
in my own thinking, so my body would no longer feel
love and death are completely indistinguishable.

3

Because he speaks passionately about Foucault's circles of power, circles
of pleasure, and does not desire women, I give a friend a frame
filled with glittering sand on which I've placed a gold maze
that imitates the shape of a small crushed snake I've set within it,
and, in the far left corner, a pale green stone mazed
with concentric circles as if it were seen through water pulsing
with its weight. Behind the stone, in a nest of fresh
red petals, the ochre heart of a drying rose
curled into itself tight as a bud. For balance,
hooked on the near right corner of the frame, a thorned seed husk
in the shape of a cross, into the stem of which an insect has bored
a perfect circle, so now it makes no sound if you shake it.
With a sprig of pyracanthas and a long black feather,
I furrow the sand so it imitates the snake's passage,
which echoes the gold coils of the maze, which echo the concentricities
of the stone and the rose. It has a name, I tell him,
as if that could contain the questions he raises.

4

Today, resting somewhere between dream and consciousness,
I heard my neighbors' voices, clear and meaningless as chimes,
felt the light draining out of the sky and did not dare open my eyes.
In my mind's eye I could see the sand falling into the furrows
I had drawn and knew that each grain falling is a cry of pain
and longing for something large and bold enough
to hold us all, entire. God.

5

A hand reaches out to me from the mirror,
the shadow of a skeleton wings, angelic,
over the tracks of my own feet.
Midwinter, all these pictures plead
for a narrator, a story.
All I can give them is this: Still Life: 40.

But my whole body aches when it sees
in an old warped photograph, black against an expanse
of bright green grass, the silhouette of a young boy.
Hidden deep in a stand of rhododendron, he waits
with one hand upraised, one drawn back close to his mouth,
as if even today he could be swept away in a rage of tenderness.

Exactly what is my body responding to, an idea, motherhood,
time, or just a fact thrown back more violently on the nervous system:
I will never love anyone as I loved him then.

my own face
se pictures. Plead
a story...
them is this: Still

whole body aches
urped photogra
een grass, t
in a stand
upraised, one draw
he could be swept

ody responding to, an idea, motherhood
rown back more violently on the nervous syste
as I loved him the

6

As we talked into the night, our outstretched legs brushed casually,
and the skin registered something both beastly and dear
about being human. I don't ignore it, but can't claim it either.
It amazes me as all small intimacies do. (From a distance the sand
slipping grain by grain into the furrows sounded then like a sleeper's
sweet suspiration of disbelief.) Today my voice sounds like a stranger's,
so deep and rough with too little said or too much. I never told him:
Five years ago there were days I was incandescent with pain.
I wanted to tear off all my clothes just to slow the burning.
Expose it as a way to deny it for what it was—just the beginning
of a purification that seems it will never end. *I don't hate men.*
I fear them with my whole being.

7

What does it mean to dream our way into the silhouette
of someone else's life? I mean, literally, to incorporate it
into our skin and nerve ends. I don't believe it is the same
as dreaming our way into our own. Although they are both,
however bold, only ideas.
See here:

A man snores in a hotel room in Bucharest.
Another man turns, enraged, and buries his face in the mattress.
In his mind, he hears his own voice, deep and reasonable:
Surely, no one could expect me to listen to this all night.
His friend, phlegm flapping like a huge gray veil
against the lungs' red alveoli, is dying
and knows it but doesn't know his friend, wildly
listening, is leaving small damp tracks in the white sheet.
They look symmetric and dark as bullet holes
in the fleshy glow of the city's reflected light.

His friend is alive, but dying. He is doing the same—on a longer
sine wave. He wills his body to relax. But the sound rakes
his ears, and he doesn't know how he can last out the night.
To calm himself, he recalls Vienna, their rented apartment,
the landlady who said, pointing to a closed door, *verboten*.
So as soon as she left, they had inspected it
more curiously than they ever had each other's body
and saw it harbored nothing, that was its mystery,
there was nothing there, it was prepared for a visitor
who had never arrived—but he had taken the room, the role
when his friend's snoring bothered him too much
and had lain alone in the cool still dark
trying to imagine what it would mean no longer to have someone

with whom to remember when life seemed simply a question
of the sharp sweet pant of desire. For years it followed them,
alleys and clubs, beaches, parks and their own bedrooms—
they could never get enough.
He lay alone in the *verboten* room, smiling fondly at the sound
of his friend's snore, muffled by doors and a long corridor,
Comforting as his own heart.

8

In a foreign country where the air is the color of terror
a woman has been abandoned by her lover.

On the walls of her small kitchen, she has pasted sagittal photographs
of the anatomy of the brain, the flawed valves of the heart.
The photographs have yellowed with heat and steam, but she keeps them
to remind herself that once she had dreams
of cause and consequence that were fixed, however bitterly.
She believed in remorse and redemption.
The woman in the kitchen pours tea, then finds herself
crouched beside the stove, the pain is like a fist
deep in her throat, she will never be free of it.
She can't even lift her hands to defend herself.
There is no point. She is alone. But the pain is so deep
the body automatically caves in—as if that could protect it.
I, the word rakes away the inside of her mouth,
I have destroyed my life.

9

Even now, the hot dry touch of his friend
comforts his skin in a way that goes beyond lust or grief,
all these fucking systems of belief, and he wants it to go on—
without the snoring. His friend is a rational man.
All he has to do is explain. His breathing is deeper now,
as if the phlegm covers his glistening red alveoli
closer than a caul, and then the crouping cough
as if he were spitting back cum, enough to make one wince
away from the scorching hand, and still he sleeps on, oblivious,
as if someone had stopped off his ears with their tongue.

10

Alone in an apartment in a foreign country
a woman stands in a marble shower stall and lifts her face
into the clean fall of water, howling.
She is not afraid of disturbing the neighbors.
They don't speak her language. Only animals do.
This is brute pain, without beginning or end,
formless as the wind. She is deafened
by the water, the steady clench and distension
of her diaphragm, which is, in itself, a kind of affirmation.
She is not so lost she doesn't know this.

Or that the pain will, like this flood of sound, crest
and recede. Repeat. It will repeat.

11

The rage is suddenly more than he can bear.
He can hear his father's voice building in his throat
and presses his mouth down to the white sheet
and begins to pant with the effort to restrain it.
They are both rational men. All he has to do is explain.
Controlling his breath, he rests with his chin on his hands
watching the searchlights strafe the drapes and the walls.
It must be close to dawn. He glances at his watch. One.
His friend strokes his arm with two fingers and smiles
and he knows in his dreams he has been mistaken
for his friend's lover miraculously recovered from the dead.
He wants to scream: *I am what I am.*
He lifts his hand until it wavers inches above his friend's mouth
and feels the air suck away from his skin as his friend's chest swells.
It takes everything he is to resist the vacuum.
The sound is incessant and loud as his own voice once was,
twelve and expelled from his chest by his father's blows.
In Bucharest, he thinks, something catching in his throat,
clearing again, *no room is verboten.* And smiles.

So he, who is forty and has never let anyone close enough
to break his heart, because he is a rational man, and kind,
and this is not the time, holds on,
but just until dawn.

12

Last night I dreamed I held an infant to my bared breast
and felt its lips close against my skin, the milk spill,
and woke relieved that desire again could speak so nakedly.

But even today, I don't understand how it is
I have come to believe in mercy.

night *I dreamed*
elt its lips close a
ok *re*lieved tha

...od...y. I don'
...ne to believe

I hurt her like an arrow...
Now I hold her thought it is our lowest point.
It is the deepest form of touch...
If the past were a glass, enough of us, each
ymol by petal, to define a lifetime.

II
THE INTELLIGENCE OF LOSS

ONCE MY MOTHER KNEW MY NAME

For Penelope

Once my mother knew my name
as she did those of violet, trillium,
cinquefoil, the poppies in Flanders' fields.
Nothing will ever feel the same.

Surely what sustains us is just this simple.
A shadow racing across a pasture
faster than thought and then we are caught
in a hot pure light. Once my mother knew my name.
I heard her, like an answer.

These nights I watch the moths cicade
through the light's halo and dream inside
the moon's perfect globe a flower unfolds
furtive and luxurious as womanhood.
Petal by petal, I assume my mother's myth
and begin the unraveling designed
to transcend time. First my name, then hers.

As a child, enthralled, bewildered,
I would watch for hours as Japanese flowers
bloomed from clam shells no larger than my thumbnail.
Mute. Huge. Blazing.
Names I believed were transformations.
I stared into the water glass as if into God's face
the equation was that exact.

Now I am left with a sensory trace deeper
than memory, the pressure of my mother's shoulder
as wordlessly we watched together. Like homecoming,
to name is to lose, reclaim. The thought threatens
to tear my mind as if it were flesh:
She knew me before I knew myself.

She doesn't know where she is any longer.
She doesn't know what makes her face clammy, wet.
As I stroke her forehead beads of sweat break inside my hand.
Glass. Water. Mother. Daughter.
Once she knew my name.
I hurt her like an answer.
Now I hold her because it is the language left to us.
It is the deepest form of worship.
If the past were a glass, enough grace settles here,
petal by petal, to define a lifetime.

THE INTELLIGENCE OF LOSS

1

When I first cupped the print in my hand I felt the simplest
relief. My mother in my red coat. She keeps recognizing
it as mine and offering to give it back. She who has always been
a relentless succession of desires so intense
you couldn't call them selfishness.
And now there is this effacement almost mystic
in its completeness. Red, she cries out.
And with each rush of sensation, like a receding tide,
remembers less. I feel a mother's rage. I want to shield her
from herself. It is an old story, inexorably
transformed.

2

Waiting for the movie to start, sitting together in the dark,
I repeat over and over the names of her children
and the order of their birth. I never seem to tire of this.
Stop only when the screen fills. But the movie makes her restless,
people appear, disappear. Weird, she says firmly as she dips
her face into her cupped hands, cheerfully meets
the eyes of the woman washing beside her in the mirror.
As we leave the theater, she looks at me sweetly and asks,
Who was your mother? She uses my given name.
She is pleased by my answer. *Did we ever live together?
Where?* I take her arm as we cross the street.
She does not brush me away as she used to.
To be abandoned and denied are different entirely.

3

All I can think about is getting us near water. I think
if I do not have something vast like that to rest my eyes on
I will die of grief. Seated there, staring out with me
at the shiftless horizon, she asks again, *Who were my children?*
I return to the car to collect the camera. From there,
I am careful to position her, in my red coat she keeps exclaiming over
and offering to return, along with the three birds in the grass,
the striae of seaweed and sand, the surf and the clean horizon
dividing the vast sea from the monochroic sky, all the elements
in such perfect internal proportion the image hums.
As I hear the shutter close, I know I am giving up something,
all those stories I have been making and remaking all my life
to try to understand why her life has been the way it has.
All this time and thought on my part and I can't give her back
the simplest thing, what it felt like to breathe deeply
on a June morning in 1950, or what it feels like
to do the same here on a California beach in September 1992.

This is a picture of what it might feel like if she knew
what was happening and could put herself in my shoes.
What haunts me is not the scale of the photograph, that feels natural
to me, the world falling away from us infinitely on either side,
but the acceptance. Can you understand?
If I had my deepest wish, we would stop right here.
She wouldn't slip an inch further away.
I would never ask anything more of her either.

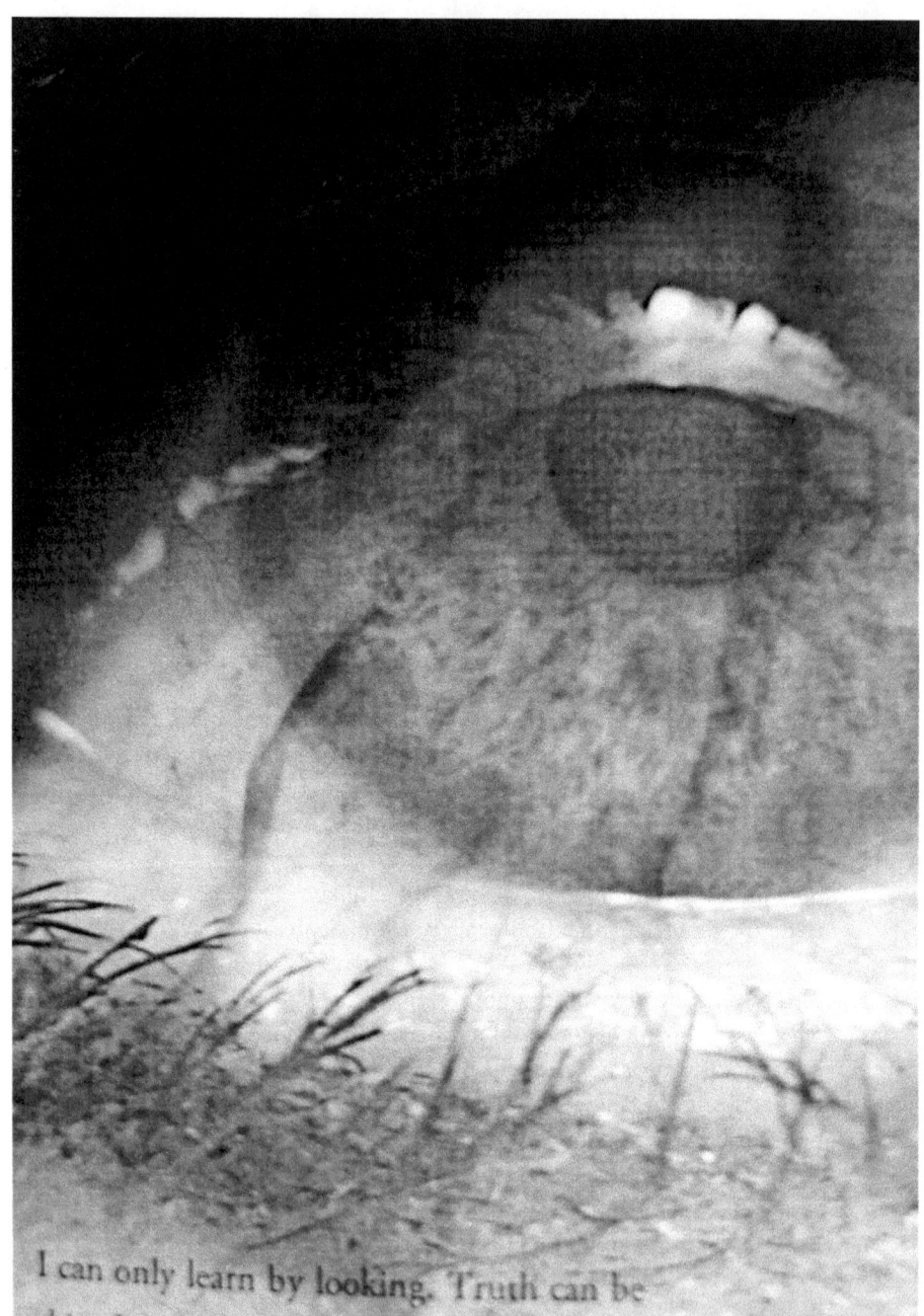

I can only learn by looking. Truth can be skin deep. Which doesn't mean we can reach it. It retreats with every word.

SKIN DEEP

1

The child is alive, flying like an angel
straight into God's face. The surf breaks
against her father's knees, foams
over the crotch of his white swim trunks.
Beneath the brim of his black hat, his eyes
are louvered, intent on the drops of water falling
singular as pearls from his daughter's feet.
One doesn't know, the way her legs bow,
if he intends to dash her to the ground
or bear her, as she is now, aloft and seraphic,
all the way to land.

I return to the image obsessively,
the luxurious graininess and flare,
as if there were something here
I can only learn by looking. Truth can be
skin deep. Which doesn't mean we can reach it.
It retreats with every word.
The father hoists the daughter aloft.
Her back arches, legs spread, in an ecstasy
of trust. The stasis is what I return for,
the water streaming in a neat cascade
from her slick skin back to its origin.

2

In the woods outside my window, the birches
flare in the first light. Here and there
I see their bark has split with the cold,
the incisions unbelievably neat, as if someone had boldly
sliced them with a scalpel, cuts deep enough
to expose, if they were flesh like us, the pleural intima.
As I pass, my hand reaches automatically
to close the fissures. What if I left well enough alone?

I return to the picture obsessively,
the photographer's equipoise, the ecstatic abandon
of the child, the father's almost professorial concentration.
I hear a man's voice saying, the detachment is almost clinical,
travesty is in the eye of the beholder.
(I am, am I, the eye of the beholder?)
Every time I look away from the book on my desk
I see the birches and I don't know what to believe.
I never did.

3

The girl's sex is sealed. Even with her legs spread
all you see is a shadow, narrow as a tendril.
The father's prick dangles limp and pale
over the waistband of the white trunks.
The horizon is a flare of light.
The decade is the fifties. You can choose the year.
The girl hears the surf as if it were
inside her head, cacophonous and sure
as the light, her father's hold on her.

For a day now, I have tried to stay exactly where I am
in relation to the picture. I know what I see
but I don't dwell on it. I focus, like the photographer,
on the naked girl, the way her feet arch toward the sea,
the undulations of her mons and diaphragm,
her obvious innocence. Truth can be skin deep.
Why need we speak of it?

4

Amid the few remaining artifacts of my mother's life,
I find slides of children's birthday parties and Halloween parades,
and, shuffled haphazardly among them, images of syphilis,
gonorrhea, leprosy, slide cultures of sporotvechosis
glowing like the moon. When I find an image of my own thigh
and right arm photographed with a purely clinical interest
against a family dishcloth, I feel relieved.

The truth, you see, can be skin deep. It can scar film
permanently with color. I try to preserve the same
relation to the image on the slide I have to the woman
I see, waking, in the mirror. Could I have spoken clearer
if I posted myself over with words?
The one that occurs to me now as I sit at my desk
and stare back at the black and white photograph
that has mesmerized me for days
would never have occurred to me then.
It doesn't belong to a girl of ten.

5

I hold the slides of my own thigh up against the window glass
so I can see my blemished childish skin against the birches.
I look at the loose dick dandling, an abandoned book,
a stranger's photograph, and somewhere inside I hear
my own voice, fully grown, daemonically clear.
You know this couldn't have happened by chance—
And at the same time I admire how high
he holds her above himself as if she need never know
where she came from, where she's going.

The truth, and herein lies its terror,
is that no one dies of violation. It requires,
for its full power, desire and trust and consciousness.
Everything, that is, we need to live.

When the ice builds under the chill auspices
of the darkest season, the wind can sing
along its farthest rim with the same clear chime
the ice itself makes breaking again in the spring.

THE CALL

When the ice builds under the chill auspices
of the darkest season, the wind can sing
along its farthest rim with the same clear chime
the ice itself makes breaking again in the spring.
Then, if my memory serves, the light blisters
the bared water until it is as thick with light as the ice
that, shattered, wind tossed, rings against the rocks.

The point is, I had forgotten, until last night I heard
what at first I thought was a flock of birds
driven by the encroaching dark to one last furious hymn
of homecoming, but then I realized there were no birds,
this eery singing was just the wind worrying the edges
of the ice and suddenly it brought to mind
the first time I had heard the same sound
and these two ideas were now yoked to one another
with some violence, and I thought, I am being asked something
large and lucid as this line of piercing yellow light on the horizon,
clean and at the same time indistinct
as the song resounding in the hollow between ice and water—
and I knew the only possible answer could be yes
and that I did not dare utter it yet
and understanding all this I felt the weight
of the water settling into the sand, the mystic lift
of ice, the flight of one bird winging black against the mauve sky,
and the strange heartbreaking graze of light on the horizon
that kept reminding me the unuttered word can be heard
and, whatever we might wish, nothing but death is final.

KOAN FOR MY SON AT TWENTY-ONE

When you meet a stranger on the path, kill the stranger.
When you meet your mother, kill your mother.
When you meet your father, kill your father.
When you meet the Buddha, kill the Buddha.

When you meet life, kill life so that when you meet death, death may enter you painlessly. We are all looking for ways to be free. Mishima. Gilgamesh. My son at twenty-one. Perhaps Satan was an angel who tried too hard, he cries, enraged, at his first serious girlfriend. Now, he recites to me a koan so bitter I cannot conceive its troubled heart.

I understand her, he says. So how can I be so angry? These days he understands rapists and murderers. He understands the child who whispers, *Papa*, to the man who boards her mother away from the world. He understands the woman who sinks, her back remorselessly straight, into the puddle of mud. He understands the rage of the man who lifts the hatchet. The child's scream that hovers in the air like Mishima's heartless koan.

The identification and pain oscillate inside him so unbearably during the movie he can no longer see. He is the woman who is drawn, resisting, to the cutting block, the daughter screaming, the man lifting the hatchet.

He is a tall young man of twenty-one sitting beside his small mother in a darkened theater in a city he may never call home.

When you meet the Buddha, kill the Buddha.
People aren't bad, he says with his impeccable moral clarity, unless they do bad things. He cuts to the heart of my horror. *I didn't mean. . .*

When he was thirteen, when we lived in a foreign country, my son pushed open my bedroom door and saw my importunate lover straddling me.

I didn't see anything, he repeated to me as he watched a Yugoslavian movie about gypsies. The colors on the screen were stained with blue, the sky and the shadows under the desolate lovers' eyes the color of blood trapped in pools under the skin. A flood plain of the heart.

It has taken me almost ten years to assimilate this scene. With my son's act, I entered something so black and complete I never thought I would live to map its contours.

When I was ten, I believe I pushed open a door and saw my father straddling a woman I loved more than my mother. But I will never know for sure. My mind refused to record any image.

Some days I believe all the paths in my psyche lead up to this impenetrable dark.

I believe what died when my son pushed open the door had to die. Everything in my life led up to that act.

When you meet the Buddha, kill the Buddha.

Why hadn't I been able to hold him back, this man whose body matched mine like a twin? When my son saw me, my life stopped. When I saw my father, my life stopped. My son and I sit together in the dark. He folds his soaking shirt in my hand and draws it to his chest. Can't you feel? he asks me.

If he loses consciousness, he will be too heavy for me to lift. I think, some wind of grief howling mindlessly through me, the truth does not blind us. It hollows us into tunnels, into vessels. My son forgives me. I would rather die than call what I learned at ten inevitable.

I looked out at my phenomenal green garden on my son's last visit home and thought, without remorse, but with an impeaching clarity, *When he was thirteen I destroyed all the security he had ever known.* This is what has come to take its place, something richer, deeper, completely unexpected. Firmer than anything I ever built to bridge the abyss inside me. Something built on my own death.

All paths lead to this dark. My life is a tunnel of pain without name. My life is a tunnel of bliss. It isn't a question of retrieving the past, it never has been. It is a question of living inside this intensity of pain and terror and abject dark that is the moment I as a child pushed open that door.

All my life I have tried to take out my own eyes. Because they caused me unbearable pain. And I did not mean harm to anyone. And caused it all the same.

All the visions are one vision. I am held in God's consciousness as if in the warm dark of the womb and I see unspeakable things being undone.

We cannot release what holds us until we take it completely in. On a mountain top, I lean over in a yogic curl. My mind is a single wave of red. My throat is blocked. I am relaxed as I gag, silently, my back to my son, who sketches, contentedly, on the cabin porch.

I see a tunnel, red, a pinpoint of dark. I know, as I lean forward, that this is what holds me back as an artist. I know this is the time to give myself over to it. To rest unresisting in the untroubled heart of this bitter, bitter koan.

...rning blackbirds tumble, shrieking, from the
... white dog trails me loyally. I am at peace.
...st presses its face against the window pane
...istortion feels normal as the shock
...eet touching cold floorboards each morning.

...understand this as an invitation
...gh I have not met you yet. *Así.* ...
...hen you do, speak to me as if...
...ture of light, as if I were an ancient hymn
...ing through the cracks in a cathedral,
...k of starlings gyring in a bitter wind,
...inning. *Así. Así y todo.*

III
SOUL HOUSE

ASÍ ES

Somewhere, a feather sifts from the rafters
in a room undisturbed by human breath for decades.
I *am* afraid.
And secure as the bats beating deeper into the sweet blue
certitude of evening. *Así. Así es.*

Tonight the moon brisks in its basket of branches
and asks of the sea, so unconscionably responsive,
everything the sea has blessed, dashed, recaptured.
Así. Así y todo.

The roof I sleep under is redder than an exposed heart.
The color burns into my brain. *Así. Así es.*
But in the dark the color is no different than that of the void
that so tenderly cradles the stars. *Así. Así y todo.*

Please, a man whispers, mortally tired
from counting his numbered days. As he speaks he feels
the dark, like the belly of an enormous beast, distend,
collapse, and he hears eternity slough just as brusquely
from his own lungs. His wife touches his fingernail,
testing something. Warm. Yes, he is still warm.
Así. Así y todo.

Language devolves and the dust rushes up
to fill the spaces the horses' hooves have gouged
in our dreams. *We are what we seem.*
I trust you to understand this invocation
in pictures, although I'm not sure I do yet.
Así. Así es.

The roof I wake under is redder than the roof of my mouth.
Why have I imagined desire can be soiled, like old money?
A knife handle cracks my sternum clean as an eggshell.
What will be revealed is both known and unknown.
A morning like any other. A wonder.
Así. Así y todo.

This morning blackbirds tumble, shrieking, from the trees.
A strange white dog trails me loyally. I am at peace. *Así.*
The past presses its face against the window pane
and the distortion feels normal as the shock
of my feet touching cold floorboards each morning. *Así. Así es.*

I trust you to understand this as an invitation
although I have not met you yet. *Así. Así es.*
But when you do, speak to me as if I were
a creature of light, as if I were an ancient hymn
slipping through the cracks in a cathedral,
a flock of starlings gyring in a bitter wind,
a beginning. *Así. Así y todo.*

SOUL HOUSE

1

It is a new theory that I hear with a shiver of recognition,
my sixth sense, like an ancient truth finally being voiced
so it feels as new as the last egg in the cache I was given at birth
falling free of the follicle, tumbling through a most intimate void,
truly innocent. Women are, this is what they say now, essentially
corruptible, or, differently accented, pure conduits to the world.
Because life is so inexplicably chancy, there are these most mysterious
lapses between the promise of the follicle and the organs
of reception, whatever enters us is free to enter us completely, slipping
through cervix, uterus, fallopian tube into that hot cavity
that houses our lung, spleen, and tumultuous heart. Today the idea
explains so much—the quiet futility that underlies all our pretenses
of defense when a man, so wanted and dreaded simultaneously,
comes close carrying the unbearably heavy weight of his loins,
rife, so rife with hope. I have housed too many souls,
I want to say and my hands reach out anyway
as if all the others were such poor approximations—
if I had known, if I had known. . . I would have waited for him
so burdened with such a pure fire he obviously yearns
and dreads to share, it lights his face and dries the skin of his huge
open hands. It is all still there, this is what I've always known,
the wildfire and remorse, bacteria and moondust, and can we ever
call alien to our deepest self what we have taken so completely in?
If we do, a friend murmurs this morning in mystic consolation,
we destroy a part of the universe as well as ourselves.
The soul is here to learn. Did it have to come, this knowledge,

with such turbulence? It's one, he said, the peace and the anguish.
In this way, you see, we marry time to the infinite,
co-creators with God. So it is not as if I lack spiritual purpose.
But my name, my name is Legion, and I would,
my love, my love, be one and your safe haven.

2

Today I grieve for every one of the children we will not bear
together, and cherish like God's sweet kiss on my forehead,
the knowledge that the promise can never arrive too late
for us to receive it or each other—but there's no life,
no life to come of it, or not as I've ever defined it,
and I grieve most deeply for what I did not know I had to give
and can only think this means that when I take you
into my body I must knowingly take everything you bring,
the farthest reaches of our galaxies too—
what else can make up for what we've lost,
and, at the same time, in the very losing,
found. How was I, God tell me, to know?
Nature is so prodigal and time so absolute
how could I have understood there is a moment
in a woman's life when they reverse their polarities,
a woman becomes infinitely empowered by all she's lost
and she gives it back like the gift of life without a second thought
as if the organ of reception were now his
and the hot, prodigal promise,
so heavy, my love, so very heavy, were my own.

                    birth
                mate void,
             ntially corruptible,

           ost mysterious la
          reception,
completely, slipping through
at hot cavity
art. Today   our preten
y that
and dreaded simultaneously,
ly heavy weight of his loins.
sed too many souls,
out anyway
r approximations--
  I would have waited f
e he obviously yearns
face and dries the skin of h
 this is what I've always kn
ria and moondust, and can
what we have taken so con
       in mystic cons

LEXICON

In the actual use of expressions we make detours, we go by side roads. We see the straight highway before us, but of course we cannot use it, because it is permanently closed.
                                        Ludwig Wittgenstein

1

Every word we speak betrays us.
There isn't one we haven't used before.
Love, desire, passion, fidelity, joy,
forever, more, most, *only you.*
There isn't one we left sacrosanct.
So, to be accurate, all we have left
are these fragments—morphemes of sense.
A yellow blanket in Tennessee backwoods.
Jasmine tea dark as bark.
The pressure of your cheek against mine
as the river flows irresistibly beneath us.
The way the pulse of a butterfly's wings,
blue red, blue red, speaks directly to my sex.
This, I must say it, is the state you have brought me to.
Across miles, I hear your breath. You are waiting
for me to match its steadiness,
some phosphorescent ebb and flow,
see, its traces mark my thighs. Alive.
Everything in me is alive to you.

2

Even at our age, the body renews itself
as the mind cannot. We've used them up.
All the words, all the turns of phrase, all the frames of thought.
Sorrow is too narrow a word for what I feel toward my own
life story. Grief and rage can't begin to encompass
the furnace of love that tempered your soul.
I built my life with no idea of you.
What faith then can I place in my own thoughts?
You must know, you whisper. You must know what a miracle
you are to me. How could a woman who has abandoned
all hope of love, know it, when it comes, as I do, for a perfect good?
I have no way to share this, except the rhythm of my breath,
the way my body opens to house your laughter,
and in that exchange, so simple and contained,
small as my physical frame, I know myself to be a source
of freedom. Nothing in me resists you.
I want. I want. I want to know you until I die.
I never thought I could feel so undividedly.
But there isn't a language I know, yet, that can hold it.
What would it mean to organize our minds around pleasure
instead of desire, around the completeness of touch
instead of the keen yearning of words, to believe
without equivocation that we are, all, children of God
that the kingdom and its promise are here now,
that we are, forever, found?

3

Pleasure is the great integrator.
It can marry without effort
irreconcilable ideas—that's why
experience has taught us to be so careful with it.
It is as daemonic as the holy.
What room, I ask you in the dusk
as you kneel over my body,
so quietly, wildly open to you,
what room do our lives leave us for purity?
Ah! And then silence as your mind
reorients to meet me just as effortlessly
as your body. Purity is what we reach with experience.
God knows, we didn't begin there.
Purity isn't innocence.
But we have no way to make the distinction.
In our ignorance, we exhausted all the words.
So there is nothing I can give you that is perfectly new,
exact as the dusk erasing our faces, marrying your hands
to my skin, nothing except what floods the silence between us,
Ah! How that breath of yours, miraculous in its sweet assurance,
makes me dream of a future— I, who thought
years ago I had severed all the nerves that fed my heart.

4

We have so many ways, every one of us, of returning
to the same place: loss. Every word betrays us.
But I would, with you, go someplace completely new.
I dream these days of embryos, placentas flowering
boldly in the dark. It is the only image that feels true
to the nature of what is happening between us.
I dream of an attachment so deep that we will never
be free of it, where desire nurtures and need feeds.
I dream of a silence so fast and so calm it can absorb
the whole century of experience that rests, unhealed,
in our cells: shattered door frames and suicide attempts
you couldn't prevent, the howl of a young husband whose wife
adores oblivion above everything, the drunken swagger
of a toddler whose mother lies dead to the world,
that ravaging mirror, love, sweet love, in which you sought
for years and years and years to know yourself. Bone knowledge.
I dream it can all be taken in. The woman who crouches
by a stove in Mexico, her whole life a single convulsion
of grief, the thousands and thousands of days I lived
within a screen of neural fire, the way, to survive, I had to cut
the nerves that guide the heart so it would beat with the strict
thoughtless measure of a stranger's cells. And the others,
I gather them in too. The father whose hands mimic the fluttering limbs
of his newborn child, the girl who holds her infant son
to her breast and stares, so fiercely, into the future.
Here in the dusk, the body renews itself without losing
anything. Ah! you say, and this sweet sea
begins to move between us, first you, then me,
as if grace were sensible and our bodies, embraced like this,
could cherish the rest, as if we understood now

that trust is the true syntax of the spirit
and, even at our age, the heart can learn
an entirely new lexicon, where all the facts
of our lives remain exactly the same
but their meaning is, forever, changed.

...any word we speak betray...
...isn't one we haven't...
...desire, passion, tide...
...movement, must...
...isn't one we let... sanct...
...to be accurate, all we have left
...these fragments—morpheuses of sense

SOMETIMES THIS DOES NOT FEEL LIKE LOVE

Sometimes this does not feel like love,
these vast tectonic plates of the psyche
slipping and sliding.
I feel to survive I must lie
immaculately still—
and then I realize, where God can enter,
God can heal.
So I draw you nearer. Nearer still.

But I am, and I am alive.
And when this cataclysm of memory is done,
I will sit quietly with you watching
the moon rise above the oaks
and think of every one of us in this world holding
such an enormous universe of feeling.

IV
FAITH

FAITH

1

I wake at the window
my hands thrumming at my chest
like trapped birds.
Immediately, you are awake
and your voice guides me back.
The Hotel Richelieu. New Orleans.
This is the moment. This is the moment.
You know me. You are making distinctions.

Hours earlier, in the dark, I rocked over you
like a bark moored on a quiet sea.
Mouth to sex. Mouth to sex.
This is the ultimate act
of redemption. Your voice
in the dark calls me back
from the moment when all trust
was broken. *Jesuschristjesuschristjesuschrist.*

These are not my own words I'm speaking.
But I do know this: the Holy Spirit
is a fierce and living thing that visits
without warning. A child mourns
with a wild, wordless thrumming.
A woman understands that more is coming.
Hotel Richelieu. New Orleans.

Three o'clock in the morning.
My skin burns from the battering
of those wings. We are not talking
about dreams. Everything is exactly
what it seems. I am not alone.
I will never be so lost you can't
find me, and, when you do, take me,
shaking, in. I trust the voice that guides me
back to you, back to me.
Where is my good book hiding?

2

Where is my good book hiding?
Where is God's love biding?
Not on the bookshelf.
Not on the landing where I stand frozen
in the Devil's stare. He smiles
and I know what it is to be known
and completely alone.

Every night I could hear him stalking,
my heartbeats marking his footsteps on the stairs.
Faster. Faster. This is how a little girl dreams
of redemption. She takes flight from the white cliffs
of Dover but there he is, on the far side of the ocean,
waiting, his hands outstretched.
One touch and her bones will blacken.
She is so tired of flying, the way her arms
have to flail at the air to keep her
just out of touch. This is how a little girl
saves herself. She throws herself to the wind.

She never dreams, she never dreams of speaking.
She will be, she will be, she will be, good.
It is only now, when I would love and be loved
by you, that I grow perfectly calm
inside the palms of a man.
But deep inside me I believe God
will bash my head in if I speak even once
of steadfast love. This must have been what he threatened,
after, when I couldn't control my breath.
That's what he must have said, so tall, so dark,
so far from where I'd fallen. His voice must have been so cold and so
hard it held, like God's, the power
of life and death. My forehead sought the inhuman

comfort of stones, and I knew the horror
of a hand I can't wash clean,
of vision severed from all feeling,
of pretending to a unity, hand wrist arm,
that only the world could see.

And hell, it's here now, in my breathing.
How long does it take for a child to die to herself
and come alive again inside a grown woman?
I know to claim my love for you
in all its richness there is no escaping
what I sought, and fought, in all its forms
so fiercely fiercely fiercely
as only a child who knew love,
before ruin, can.

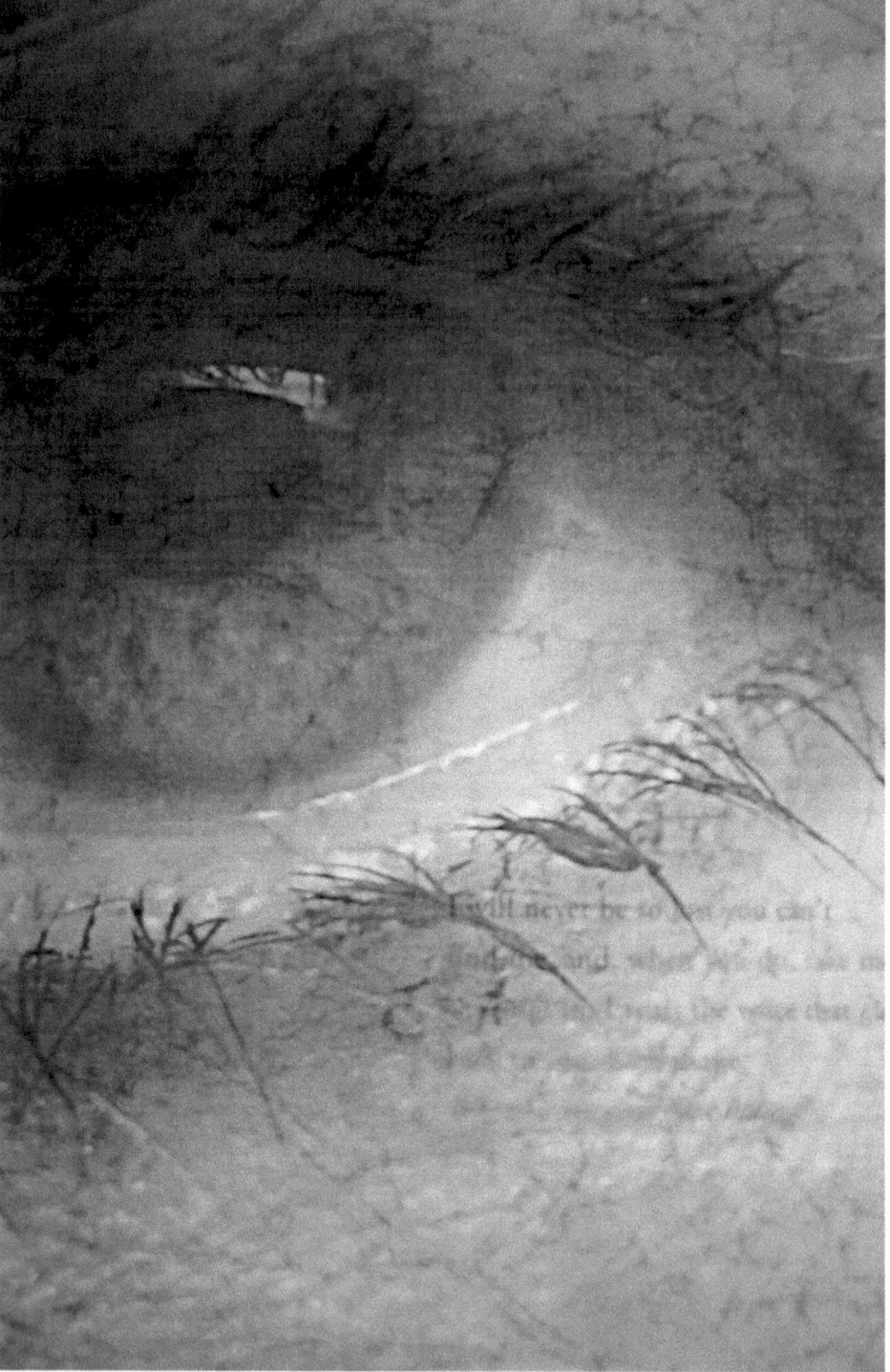

3

Sense is invidious.
A veil comes down.
This is the end of language
but not of sound.

Two little girls are in my head.
One is alive and one is dead.
Her breath doesn't trouble the forest floor.
She is no more.
The other rolls her head on a stone.
Alone. Alone. Alone. Alone.

Terror has no words.

4

How can I tell a good man
from a bad one?
The smell. The smell.
The swell. The swell.
This never happened.

If we can't cherish the origin
of terror, it becomes invincible
as water, seeps through everything
we make to contain it.
Names like good and bad,
love and hate, alive and dead.
It absorbs everything and we
at last are one electrical storm.
Wild mother. Wild child.

Sound allies an infant's monotonous sorrow,
the keening of a violated girl of seven,
and the love a woman of forty-six makes
in a sea of undreamed tenderness.

I want to bash God's head in.
I don't ever want to forgive him.
Sin is a meaningless word
for a stranger in the woods
to a girl whose head comes no higher
than his belt buckle.
How can I tell what is real
what is horror? Terror seeps
into my thoughts like adrenalin
into my muscles and gut.
I love you so much.

5

There is an explosion in my head.
One is alive. The other is dead.
What have they done to my eyes?
I am alive. I am alive.
Terrible man.
I am. I am.
Clean my hand. Clean my hand.
My forehead stings.
Rings with sting.
Sound makes it all happen again.
The devil climbs the stairs
from night to morning.
Where is my good book hiding?
The cactus have spines.

The spines fly.
I am alive. I am alive.
My skin is broken. Open.
This never happened.
We lie through our teeth.
And the devil speaks
with a forked tongue,
half old, half young,
half cold, half dumb.

6

A veil descends.
This is the end of language
but not of sound.
Forest. Floor. Forest. Floor.
There is no mystery here.
What, once, happened to me
is clear in the breathing,
the ghastly clarity of the keening.
Mystery. Meaning. Mystery. Meaning.
Our parents tear our hearts
and lock us out of sight.
But a stranger hides God from us.
A stranger drives his sex
deep into my mind.
An act repeated, here and there,
by lovers over the years.

And then there is this one
whose sex I take willingly
into my mouth and I think
I can be fed by his hesitant flesh
and then it all comes out,
the ruin and confusion.
Who, we wonder, as she keens
so clearly in the dark, knows enough
to comfort her.

She is lying very still
waiting for hell.
Robin Redbreast
is her headrest.

sought, and fought... in all its forms
to concede the pain fiercely
as one who no longer knew love,
before ruin.

7

What's happening?
I cannot see.

What do you hear?
She isn't there.

What do you feel?
This isn't real.

Why are you crying?
I'm lying. I'm lying.

Chicken Little didn't give a fiddle
for the truth.

But you?
There are two of us.

One you can trust.
One you mustn't.

Which one is that?
Can you wash my hand off?

Which one?
The right one. The right one.

Gasping in the shower
for the truth that will never come
clear to me, never come clean.

8

Terror has no words.
Crazy rhyme locks me in time.
Language is my life line.

She is lying very still
waiting for hell.
Robin Redbreast
is her headrest.

Never let him in your head
or you'll be dead.
You'll be dead.

Language is my lifeline.
It means I have to leave her there
to die. Terror has no words,
no cure. So I remember nothing.

Blood is red.
The girl is dead.
She never bled.
She never said
what happened.

Where was my good book hiding?
Jesuschristjesuschristjesuschrist.
O deary deary me, cried the woman at the stile.
This is none of I. *This is none of I.*

9

Mother of the universe—
I curse. I curse.
But he curses faster, quieter, first.
Jesuschristjesuschristjesuschrist.

Mother of the universe
you have great powers
of creation and destruction.
And I am your child.
I am your child.

A stranger comes upon a little girl
in the woods and rapes her.
This is just a fact.
There is no taking it back.

And forty years later a man comes to a woman
after thousands and thousands and thousands of days
of isolation and wakes her.
This too is true.

What mystery reverberates between
these two realities. My quiet house stirs
with invisible currents and my prayer wavers
like a single flame, flickering, steadying,
flickering again: *Mother of destruction,
help me love.*

Mother of the ...
you have great power ...
of creation and destruction.
And I am your child
I am your child

10

If you let him in your head,
you'll be dead.
You'll be dead.

Horrible thought.
Horrible thought.
Daddy's girl.
Horrible thought.
Pearl without—
Horrible thought.
World without—
Horrible thought.
Frightened, frightened,
the cataclysm of air—
beware, beware.
No. No. Oh no. No.
Pearl without—
No. No. Oh no. No.
World without—
No. No. Oh no. No.
Terror without—
Nonononono. No. No.
I want to die.
Horrible thought.
I want to die.
Horrible thought.
I want to die.
Horrible thought.
Horrible thought.
Horrible thought.

But I am, and I am alive.
And when this cataclysm of memory is done,
I will sit quietly with you watching
the moon rise above the oaks
and think of every one of us in this world holding
such an enormous universe of feeling.
Then I will ask you back into my bed
and will open my robe and disclose
this body that can hold such inconceivable pain
and still desire and be desired by you.

11

These breaths go on and on
and on and on and on.
I would put a stop to them,
No No Oh no No,
if I could, now.
But if I do I lose the words,
so few, so small, so soft, all
a little girl knew to call
herself back from the dead—
Healing is taking in the dreadful sense
she made of it so very long ago
as if it were new knowledge, mutable.

Jesuschristjesuschristjesuschrist.
This is what he said.
I don't believe he left any record in my head
of his face, his name. He was a stranger
who came upon me in the woods when I was seven.
I was carrying my new book of nursery rhymes.
I loved it very much. Its heft made me feel almost adult.
It was my birthday present.

So all this must have taken place in the fall.
England. I had just learned to read.
By Christmas Eve, on the landing, I would be able
to make that fatal metathesis: Santa is Satan.
But I would pretend for years and years and years
to believe in all the terms the world calls good.
Santa is good. God is good. Love is good.
Trust is good. Touch is good. Touch is trust.
I love you so much.

It is not inconceivable that he was,
Jesuschristjesuschristjesuschrist,
as his words implied, a man of God.
Horrible thought. Horrible thought. Horrible thought.

12

When I first saw you, your hands folded
above your waist, just like a priest,
I couldn't take my eyes from them.
I stood there, speaking glibly,
mesmerized by the unspeakable thought:
I want to be inside them.

All of me wanted, wants, to be inside them
and to call them good. What haunts me now
is that to reclaim my soul
I must know once she was whole
and some one man tore
mind from skin, beginning from end,
sight from feeling, word from breath
and left her, breath burbling like blood
through her fingers, to make her private peace
with the unspeakable.

Out of such rifts artists are born.
But we are talking now of steadfast human love
between a man and a woman and I don't know how
that applies, can possibly apply to me—
if being a child of God means
being a daughter of destruction.

Blood does not go cold in a single second.
That shift, trust to terror, is unbearable to recall.
It exists, beyond words, in my mind and in my muscles.
It came upon me once again when you said,
I would have liked to have known you as little girl,

and I answered without thinking, *She didn't suffer.*
But when you held me, my arms turned to ice.
This is what it means to be fully alive and unresisting.

Blood does not go cold in a single second.
Would it have been worse to have nothing
to lose? Little girls do not choose
to have worlds of meaning explode
inside their heads. But I, who am not a child,
who never said, who never bled, whose breath spills
now like water through my laced hands, whose agent
am I, really? If I spoke, *no, oh no, oh no oh no,* now,
would you, really, hear me?

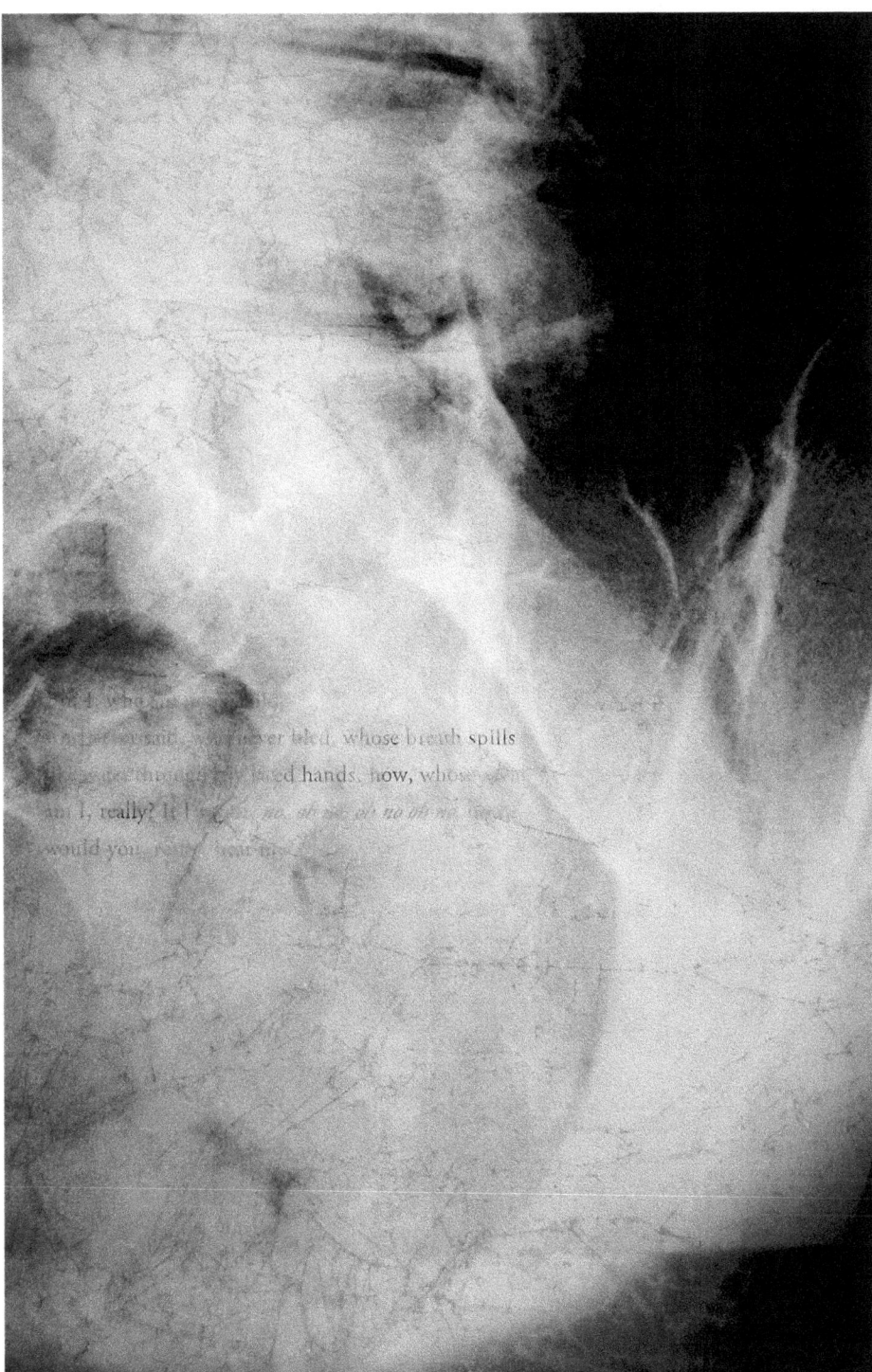

did. We did.

inking, without stint,
ke our own children
t, our own breath
od.
ill be giv
n

ATTACHMENT

We discover ourselves in our mothers' faces,
the devotion we feel toward the breast.
This is the essential welcome that denied
we would never survive. And we did. We did.
Its simplicity is its mystery.
To give. Receive. Without thinking, without stint.
It embraces us again when we take our own children
into our hands and our hearts quiet, our own breath
becomes the essential promise:
Seek and you shall find. Ask and it will be given to you.
And now, as adults, we've found it again
in the sensual continuum between us.
I touch your breastbone with my fingertips
and something passes between us, back and forth,
back and forth, that has the sweet trace
of eternity in it. Dare we call this love?
It is as quiet as a single leaf falling
to the forest floor, a moth settling on a door,
a prayer, without words, heard.

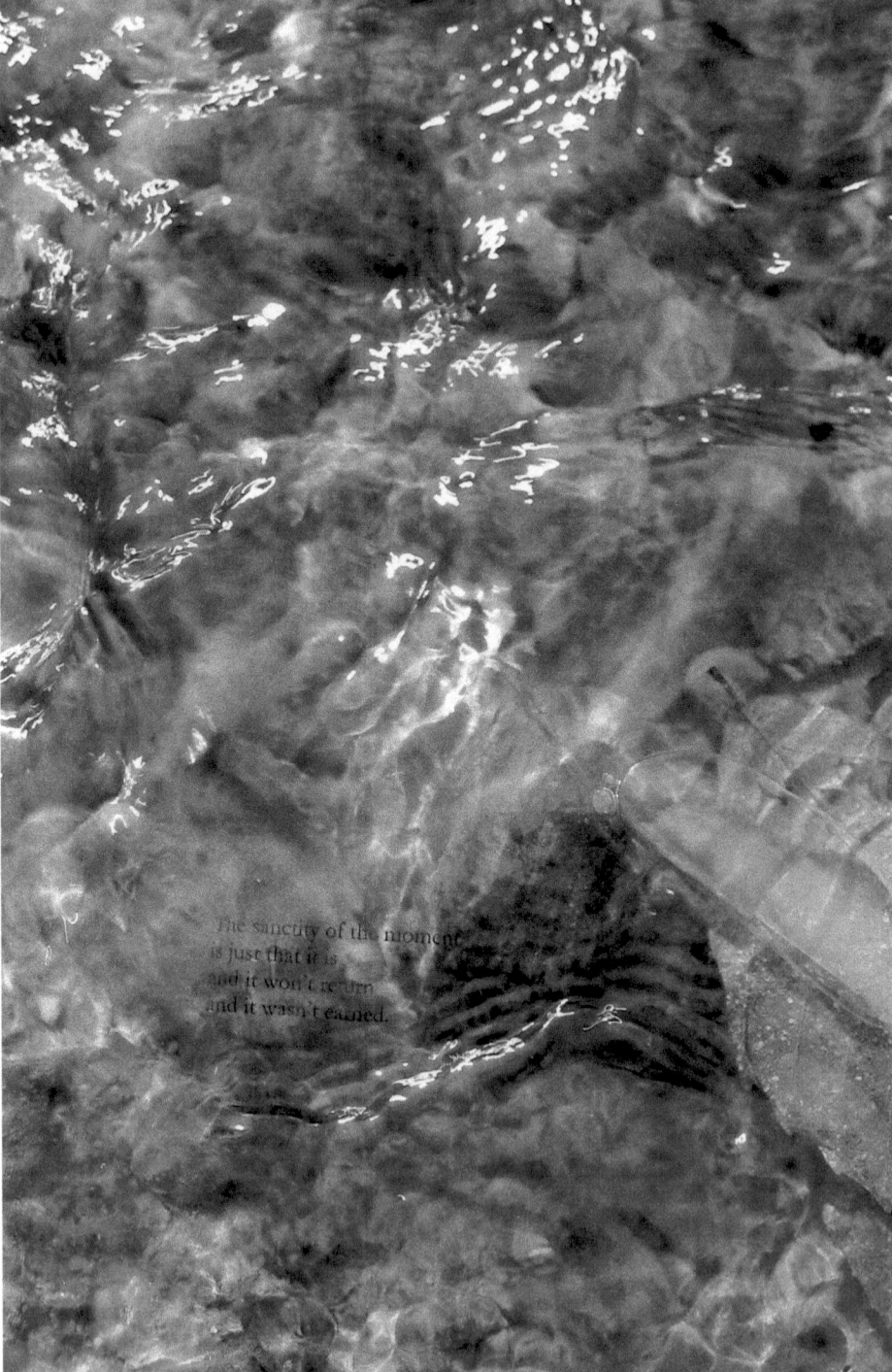

The sanctity of the moment
is just that it is
and it won't return
and it wasn't earned.

THE SANCTITY OF THE MOMENT

The sanctity of the moment
is just that it is
and it won't return
and it wasn't earned.
How can we rest serenely
in what we must give up?
The mind distorts time,
that savage metronome,
because it is all we know
of love and sorrow, this holding
pattern, growing old, so old
and we want to know what
is pushing us, what is drawing us,
and what is letting us, time and time
and time again, go
as if we were just thoughts
not flesh and blood and something,
some sweet something
that wants to take hold forever—
like the child in the womb who never dreams
that what is both food and breath to her,
her now and her forever,
will ever be severed.

to believe we've arrived
at the epicenter of our life together,
that we have come to a point
of perfect equipoise
and that we can stay here
forever, in this peace
so sure, so cellular we know
we could never dream it up

BOOK IV: 2000-2009

AUGURY, OMEN

I AM WAITING

A bird cries once, harsh and crude,
fearlessly ripping the *tela*
of sleep. On the street below
women murmur in Kachikel.
The sun disperses shadow
hours before the clock turns
night to day. We unpacked
our suitcases days ago but I am
still waiting for my body to arrive.
It defies categories like now, home,
marriage, nation, tame, wild,
work, travel, child, or die.
It measures time with a wild precision.
Tuk. Tuk. Galop. Galop.
Women murmur in Kachikel.
The sun flows up the crumpled
sheet under which I am still,
waiting for my body to arrive
in its own sweet time.
Tuk. Tuk.
Galop.
Galop.

SIN TITULO

Strangely familiar. Brutally shocking.
We have been here before
our mind assures us. Before
our bodies knew the truth
of their own dying, immanence.
We are so much younger now.
A lifetime, it's all we ever have, to catch up,
touch by touch by touch, like a child
swaddled in a *rebozo*, constantly adjusting
to her mother's motion. Strangely familiar.
Brutally shocking. Under the broad leaves
that flourish in the *campo*—plastic bags, bottles,
molding teddy bears, wet cardboard,
dirty rags. *Hectárea* after hectare. Foliage.
Trash. Hectare after *hectárea*. Trash.
Foliage. There's no separating it out
into beauty, squalor. It's like the wood soot
that every morning floats free
of the shack in the compound next door
where a woman barefoot on a dirt floor
slowly stirs *atole* over a wood fire.
It rises, lilts like snow over our electric fence,
sifts through the red petals of the bougainvillea,
and settles here in our hair, on our hands,
life's silky, staining patina. As strangely familiar
as the volcanoes that loom, green, hazy, inevitable,
over all our walls. As brutally shocking.
A lifetime, it's all we ever have, to catch up.
Touch by touch by touch. Hectare
after *hectárea*. Love. Loss. Love.

SOME SILENCES ARE LIKE SILK

Others hold at their center, like the emptiness of air,
a high celestial humming.

Some are muffled, like mauve shadows traveling through wax,
or a foetus' cry through a sealed cervix.

Some are muffling, as if we are trying to force our soul's last breath
through mouths thick with cotton batting.

Some are light, elevating, as if the air on the outside
of our skin and the white energy inside are one, indivisible,
a sure, redeeming simplicity on which all else is founded.

And there are others, like the one between us now,
that feels, some days, thick as a fog bank seen from an impassible distance,

thick as the walls of churches in Antigua ruptured by earthquake
before they succored a single true believer.

Or the one austere as a single unspoken thread running
through fifteen internal monologues conducted simultaneously.

This thought shelters motionless under the roof of my mouth:
Without me, you would not exist.

This is what my skin hears: *Yes. What of it?*

This thought shelters motionless under the rock.
Without me, you would not exist.

This is what my skin hears: *Yes. What of it?*

THERE IS A MOMENT DEEP IN THE NIGHT

There is a moment deep in the night
when the whole *pueblo* of Jocotenango
lies dreamless, still. Not a hope,
a yearning, a coming clear anywhere.
It wakes me every night,
this moment of pure stillness.
Unmoving. Human to its core.
It isn't despair.
It isn't death.
It can be taken in. Change us.

So, waking, my ears now have a point of comparison
different from the sweet devouring ringing
that accompanies me everywhere, my first prayer.

A place from which the soft chuffing
of women's voices, the piercing lament
of the songbirds, the rumbling
of cycles and buses, the clip clop
of horses trotting on cobblestones,
the trumpets of mariachis, the dangerous thrum
of a mosquito or an earthquake—

A place from which the rustle
of a bottle brush tree
or bougainvillea, the inconsolable cries

of a child next door, the insistent tap of hammers,
mesmerizing incantations of evangelicals,
the slap of hands *tortillando*, the hiss
of oil on a metal lid,
the crackle of kindling—

all take lasting meaning.

And the delicate etching everywhere

SHOULDER TO SHOULDER

we grow older.
Positioned this way,
sharing a vantage point,
we can't see each other,
must orient by oscillations in the rhythm
of our breaths, the heats of our separate skins.
Such a shimmer, a shiver
of the most basic knowledge.
But when we turn, we can't see
each other, only age
engraved on a stranger's face.
Who is this sharing our bed,
our creased pillow, our space?
And this delicate etching everywhere—
how did it get there?
As if angels had left their indelible scribbles
on our essential being. Notes we've never read—
we've been so busy watching sunsets
over Nosara, Laguna Beach, Puerto Escondido,
crossing Lago de Atitlán in frail *lanchas*,
the dun waters of Rio de La Plata in hydrofoils,
sipping Malbec in Buenos Aires,
worshipping the African queens who glide through
our bank in Atlanta, packing, unpacking, lighting candles,
calling children, making friends, making,
in our own long, luxurious, inconsequent
way, home.

LIKE BLOOD IN THE VENA CAVA

1

It returns with a slur
like blood rising
in the vena cava, effortless
return for all that pushing, pressing,
striving *out*. My father
tucked under my old red cloak
to protect him from biting April cold
doesn't know who's propelling his wheelchair.
He's obsessed with the logistics
of picking Heather up at the airport.
"She's here. Behind you. Pushing."
My heart stretches painfully.
It's the first time he's revealed
he doesn't know me from Eve.
"You're taking her back to the airport soon."

I glimpse us in a shop window.
My own cloak flared dangerously
and caught in the wheels,
so I traded him for his own.
No one would know.
It looks tailored for me.
Who would have guessed
I would want it so cleanly, keenly?

2

Ahead, I see Trinity Church,
where fifteen years ago I sought
comfort before flying to California
to commit my demented mother.
How fitting, I think, to take him here too
in person, not spirit—
he who so fears the judgment
of a God whose existence
he can't relinquish or accept.

Beside the path, a woman stands
stock-still before a cairn. She clutches
a box of rocks against her small breasts.
She walks three steps. Kneels.
Sets a stone. Rises. Retreats. Repeats
the cycle. Mesmerized, I photograph each step.
"Did you get that too?" asks a passer-by.
The handwritten sign explains this act
is both art and protest. On a daily basis.

My trips to visit my father
are now never more than a day.
Bi-annual at best. They add up.
Everything adds up.
Love. Lies. Interest. Sweet grief.

3

For the last day, truck drivers
have been shouting out tips
on how to manage the wheelchair
over steep curbs, pedestrians have swerved
or opened doors like maitre d's.
I back us up the ramp to the church
but the doors open outward,
and I almost lose my father,
so dementedly patient and frail,
as I release my grasp on his chair
to tug the door out and pull us back
from the spring chill. Only to be greeted
by yet another transparent set
of expelling doors.

A twenty-something, blonde
and blandly privileged, watches me
indifferently as I struggle to open
these doors too without propelling
my poor father back out the last.
I pause, take in the dour oak doors,
sealed, of the sanctuary, her tour sign.
She inspects her manicure.
"You can't go in there. There's a service.
You'd be disruptive."

The rage rises effortlessly, like blood
in the vena cava. "What exactly
do you mean?" I ask and let the glass
slip slowly closed. She gapes, thoughtless
as a fish. "Next?" my father asks
with surreal cheer.

4

When again we crisscross Copley Square,
an hour later, my father suddenly straightens,
exclaims, *Something happened back there.*
He sounds urgent, tentative.
I reach forward and rub his shoulder.
Something. Something the kindness
of booksellers and passers-by can't assuage.
The way this day can't assuage the choices
made over an entire lifetime,
the open questions, harsh consequences,
or my desire we both come to rest
in what can truly free us, past and future.
"A surge," I tell him. "Nothing more."
A surge of something pure. It matters
how we say good-bye. Try by try by try.

BROWN RECLUSE

The young man has bangs, blonde,
that slip and slide over a boy's
unmarked forehead, and a thin
silver ring that pouts
from his lower lip.
He's carded wherever he goes.
He comes from a town called Alma,
Baptist, where they don't speak Spanish.
He has a phobia of spiders
and a fascination with the older women
in the van whose lives are so different
from those of the girls he knew in high school
for whom, even in this day, at his age,
biology remains destiny. Vistas
open for him as he listens, chimes
in confidently, telling a vibrant
woman of seventy-six her life story
is a love story, not a how-to book
on dying.

Later, he confides,
A brown recluse bit me once
on my neck and there was a black
spot, like a pen dot, at the center,
a red halo surrounding it, and the next day,
that halo was solid black, and another halo
like the flare around an eclipse, surrounded it,
and then— He has one
distant girlfriend and an immediate need

to write. Words excite him the way they
encapsulate, re-encapsulate, their implications
expanding infinitely. He also knows that flesh
and what attacks it don't behave that way
and insists on the contradiction. "I have a terrible
fear," he says. "I had it before. Even so, I can't
bring myself to kill them. I don't know why."

AUGURY, OMEN

There is a groan, my own,
I'm trying to grow into
but it defies everything
I want to believe about
growing.

It comes at night before
I'm sleeping, when my hands
relax their hold and the book
I'm reading begins to list
toward my chest.

Then this sound, so dark
and guttural, spills free of me
as if someone were lost deep
in a labyrinth of limestone
caverns, calling

on what they can't name,
can't dream, can't live without.
The dead might make a sound like this
as the coffin latches, and they settle
the very last of their doubts, debts.

FLIGHT

In my childhood dreams, I winged it
arduously from the tall white cliffs
of Dover to the Atlantic seaboard,
flat as a map, pink as a continent.
The devil, black as night, ran
the blushing brink, fingers growing
when he sighted my faltering wings,
reached to grasp my rasping body.

I no longer see the world in two
dimensions, or in black and white.
I have no dreams of flying.
But I walk the brink of the Atlantic
mesmerized by the gleam
on the wet sand, how faithfully it reflects
the shifting sky, cool blue
to blushing rose. Then, when I least
expect it, the sky thrums
carmine and the fire won't die
until I raise my eyes, come
to standstill.

Now it strikes me, watching pelicans
glide just above the slow surf,
how high and vivid were the waves
before that cardboard continent,
how real the spasms in the back
of the little girl I once was, trying
with all her might to get safe.

All she knew was how to bear down,
not how to ride the wind, how to sense
that gracious space between
the rising heat of the earth
and the steady lure of gravity,
how to find in that mysterious
intersect of indifferent forces,
the most intimate of joys.

I feel it now, watching how perfectly
the pelicans calibrate their glide,
less than a wing's breadth above
the water, and the gulls their sweep,
even closer, over sand,
and I remember how, in the still
of the night, your breath matching
itself to mine in the dark,
just there, just close enough
to hear, nothing more,
something in me lifted,
weightless, freed to follow
the earth's sweet sweep. Again.

this beautiful woman who will never
be my daughter but whose existence
matters to me as if the mitochondria
of my mother's mother's mother
had a future in her. She flowed

I SEE DEATH IN MY FUTURE

1

Prednisone, doxycycline, zyrtec.
The prescriptions flutter as I talk.
I can't get to the pharmacy fast enough.
My wrist is thick and shiny
as my father-in-law's ankles,
the inflammation tracks the vein
from wrist to elbow as if
there were intention here.
Haste. At first I thought I dreamt it,
the bite on the back of my neck,
then the ones down my hand, wrist,
and under my breast. In the surreal
fluorescent glow of a hotel room,
four-thirty on the morning of the Day
of the Innocents, I saw
fears I didn't know I had
were real and red and spreading.

Unlike the eerie and fascinating wounds
my daughter forever at one remove
wore on her cheek and neck
hours earlier to celebrate her engagement.
Those were exquisitely positioned
and colored in by her best friend,
who came herself in a blonde wig
and vivid green Jackie suit,
dashed with blood, punctuated
here and there by blackbirds.

She flowed in a Twenties bridal dress
on that night of ghosts (that opens
into the day of saints and dead babies),
this beautiful woman who will never
be my daughter but whose existence
matters to me as if the mitochondria
of my mother's mother's mother
had a future in her. She flowed
into her own future, flaunting
those parodies of wound on her face,
carrying secretly the knowledge
that the real ones have,
at long last, healed.

Bereft by so many deaths between
fifteen and twenty—maternal
grandmother, grandfather,
uncle, mother too,
and my living presence
possibly for years the keenest
of her bereavings. But that night,
my attention was a gift received,
and her own history a life-giving stream
that pulsed around her radiant body
as easily as her pleated dress.

How then could I, falling asleep counting
our blessings, wake to these crazy welts?

2

Two days later, on the Day of the Dead,
alone in my car in a parking garage
in Georgia, I back out without
warning and jar another car.
Suddenly my attention coheres,
I slip free, caress the unmarred fenders
of both cars, and approach
a driver's window which an older woman
with large glasses and jet black hair,
eyes still fixed straight ahead,
has rolled down in anticipation.

I grip the sill, abjectly contrite, and nod
at the white-haired man beside her.
Slowly she swivels her head,
places the softest hand I've ever felt
over my own. *I know,* she says
and holds me whole with magnified eyes,
smiles. *Let it go.*

She faces forward again, her hands
exactly balanced on the wheel.
I wonder what she is here for, a daughter
with breast cancer, a husband facing bypass,
a new grandchild, or her own destiny.
"You first," I say, and she nods,
never taking her eyes off the windshield,
the dull gray wall behind it.
Stepping back, I still feel the balm
of her touch and fall in love
with her perfect carriage.

As I follow her out the garage, in a descending
spiral, on this, the Day of the Dead,
the one for the rest of us, we vast
majority whose business is messy,
unfinished, unpredictable and
salvific, I practice her carriage,
my hands poised, just so, on either side
of the steering wheel, my eyes fixed
dead ahead, turn after turn, and I imagine
that my own touch could feel that soothing
to a total stranger, that death herself
might greet me, just so, with a touch
that brings me back, fully known,
into the flow of my whole life.

who gives me, just so, with a touch
that brings me back, fully known,
into the flow of my whole life.

REASONABLE EXPECTATIONS

It looks like a mitzvah
these early morning visits
I make with a friend
to the oncology center, chic
as a spa, where there isn't
an orderly, volunteer, receptionist,
nurse, doctor or valet who doesn't
have the time for a genuine
smile, a sensuous touch
as they guide her from one
station of loss to another.
My friend is a statistician, lapsed
Mennonite, who believes religiously
in the actuarial table she read
two decades ago that told her
her life expectancy was close
to a century if she lived to seventy.
She's receiving, at seventy-three,
treatment for a second form of cancer,
but earnestly questions her young
doctor about rare side-effects
that appear ten years out. *I expect*,
she says, in a voice that has always
sounded creaky with age, *to live
thirty more years.* The young doctor
holds her gaze, permits
a real smile to quiver
in the corners of her lips and nods
her assent. *I know those figures.*

ABSENT-MINDEDNESS

Woman ascending, descending,
ascending, descending a stair.
Nu or dressed, she
could be me. Often is.
Some clear intent impels
me to move before words,
inner or outer, or even
the faintest image. But I am pure
purpose as I climb,
like a cheetah racing over veldt,
and then there is this moment, pausing
perfectly blank, in the sunlit upper story,
unstoried, when I'm free to breathe
in the autumn air, ardently
empty and replete—
or entering the basement studio
free to study what awaits me
in the gray light as if it were my own
brain smoothed clean of everything
engraved there so assiduously, eagerly,
hopelessly, over more decades than fit
on a single hand. My fingers itch
with eagerness, but I play
the same game I play with
my young granddaughter's skin,
running my palm as close as I can
to the surface without touching, without
changing anything but my own electrical give
and take. *Awake.*

FORTUNES

Today I planned to read the red leaves
that the Japanese maple of my Vietnamese
neighbor, Mr. Lee, has distributed
so prodigally and impartially
across our two lawns—
an area Mr. Lee mows all year
with a mower that rattles
his small, frail frame like the aftershock
of the bombs of his youth. When he pauses,
his smile, free of any teeth, anoints me.
Today, as if he were bearing a silver
tray, he carries out to me a copy
of his daughter's medical school
diploma. "She have real one.
Houston." As we read, we burnish
this precious facsimile
with our breath.

This *was* my plan: First to spell out our fortunes
in the happenstance of those red leaves glistening
with a week's rain. Then to burn
facsimiles of my own poems safely contained
within their plundered compass, decades
transforming into smoke and real promises.
Red. So read.

Instead I sit facing you in the swinging chairs
we brought back from Guatemala
sometime in our dozen years together.
Cumpliendo today the first week

de mi año sesenta, my body expands
to hold the anguish in my son's voice.
States away, decades dissolving,
the rush to comfort, encompass was
as raw as it was at twenty-one,
I tell you, who share my present
fully, but never my past.

We rock, you and I, in some generous
holding pattern and the pain builds
like breath, a mushroom cloud, then dissolves
into my skin—and this shared rhythm.

My son, *cumpliendo* today the first month
of his *año treinta y ocho*, is almost as old
as I was when he left for college.
He bikes for a living. He likes it.
He's married. Childless.
But today some cherished bubble shattered,
some crucial denial, and the glass,
broken and merciless, covers every inch
of the only still and solid ground
from which he can move his world.
He doesn't know what to do.
All his options look bloodied.

I've been there too.

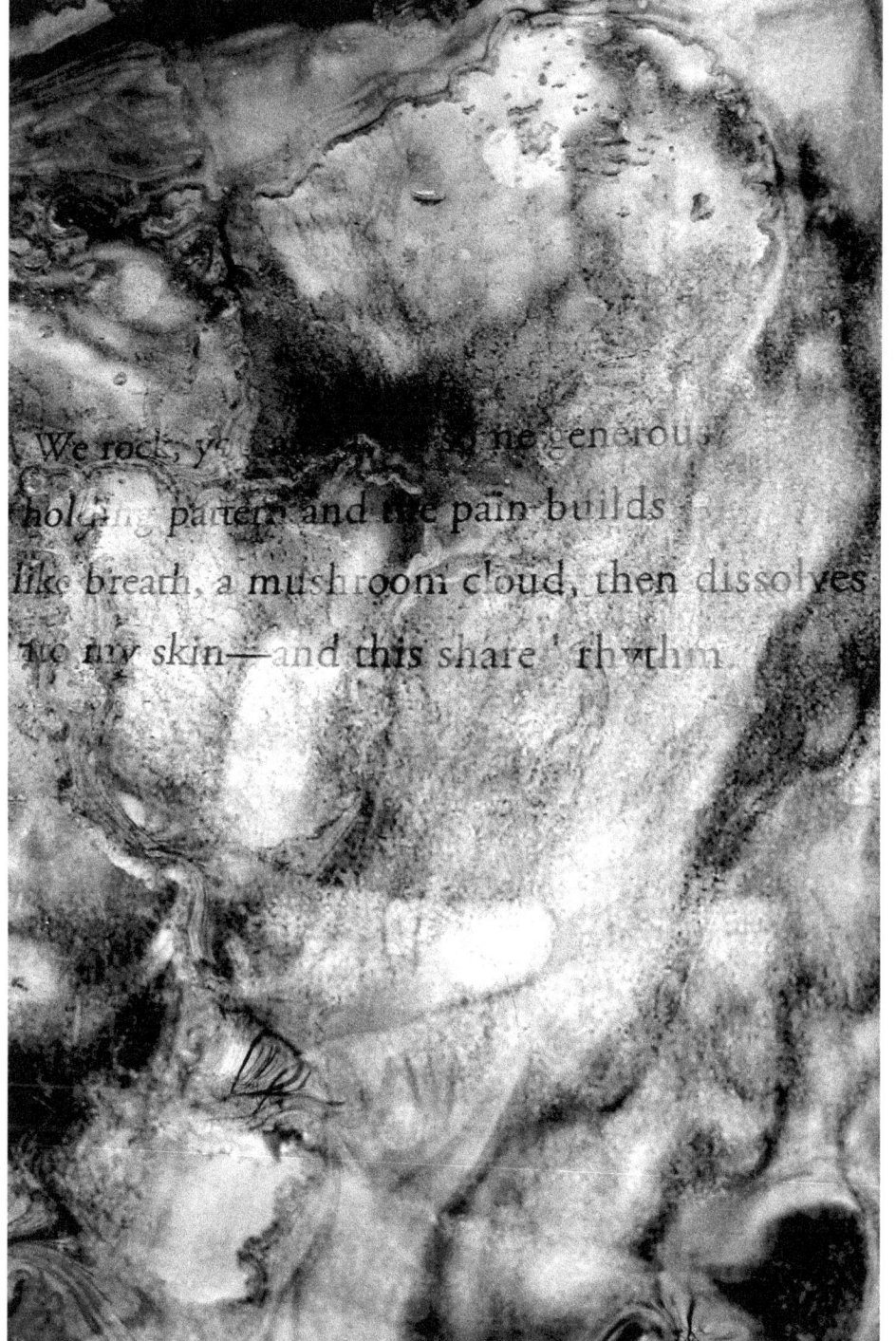

BURDENS

When the nurse tells her,
my good friend feels
her one good ear, now
fluid-filled, has failed her.
She's too old to start reading lips
but she looks at the woman's
mouth, how the lipstick
has scabbed at the peaks
of her upper lip, how her tongue
touches the inside of her lower one
as she begins to speak again,
and my friend Sybil gets it now
and yells out—and then,
the nurse has her hand on her shoulder,
is leaning into her face as if to kiss
her smack on the lips and for one minute
her good ear clears and she hears her say,
"Hold it together. Your daughter
needs you."

The only other words she hears
as clearly are her daughter's,
the way she keeps saying her husband's
name, keeps repeating like a mantra:
I loved my life. I *loved* my life.
The two young sons. The husband
whose heart just stopped one morning
a month shy of his fortieth birthday.

Stopped a full decade before the age
my friend was when she left
the mirrored bathrooms and miserable
boudoir of her long, unlamented marriage.

I loved my life, her daughter sobs
into her shoulder and the words
could have been her own the winter
before, sick with flu, an injured shoulder,
so clear that if this was what was left
to her—no scull skimming on the river, no
intensity, no zest, nine friends checking out
of existence in eleven months—she wasn't
making promises. Her children didn't need
to be burdened with her despair. But she knew
what she had had and what had escaped her,
precious as breath. So she had set a time limit.
Conditions. But here she is, holding her daughter
more tenderly and closer than she ever has,
bearing her full weight, murmuring,
"Let it out. Let it all out. Remember
the children, how much they need you."
Her daughter shakes uncontrollably.
Sybil absorbs it all. She feels her own lips
form words, feels her breath leaving.
The sound in her ears is like thunder
and snowfall, sandstorm and dew.

IT IS WHAT IT IS

The assassinations of my childhood
pass without mention this Sunday in November
in newspapers filled with the aftermath
of Fort Hood, suicide bombers in Kabul
and Peshawar. In the window to my right,
I see a few butter-yellow leaves,
bare branches, green ivy snaking
its way to the top of tall poplars and oaks
with small, dangerously friable root holds.
And to my left, oaks in full foliage, magnolias
whose split pods rain vivid red seeds
on empty flower beds. Yesterday
I set my own words on fire.

I'm fed these days by something words
can't contain but need to be
included in, changed by
their material association with—
clay, paper, fire, smoke, leaf,
concrete, spent match, x-ray, fresh
and salt water, cloud bank, sand,
skin, bark, dirt, stones, moss
and the orange box in which my father
faithfully stored all the manuscripts
I shared with him over half a century,

It is what it is, my friend Shahidah
repeats whenever I see her and these words
now feel as if they're engraving in my mind,

flowering in my heart, adding density
to my bones, thinning blood so
my stories won't clot, stop.
It is what it is: Sharif's
left leg numbed by diabetes,
the open sores from first, second and third degree
burns on his feet he never felt and that she
patiently watched heal, October to June,
learning something in the process
of the perdurable power of healing
and raw time. I set fire again
to paper, the flame doesn't waver,
it blotches, sends dark devouring stains
before itself, transmuting the black ink to silver.

The paper shatters into a fretwork of ash,
through which I see real leaves, red, brown
and butter-yellow, still wet from the last storm,
and I hear a new story forming: He kept
my truth. Locked off in a small orange box,
he kept my truth. Now, waiting, hearing these words
in new relation, I also hear our wind chimes ring
batted by a sudden gust and see in the left window
yellow leaves soar and fall like small finches.

I shared. He hoarded. I shared. He treasured.
I shared in words he had no power to touch,
mold, use to his own advantage, shared in stories
that kept reaching for the air between
bars.

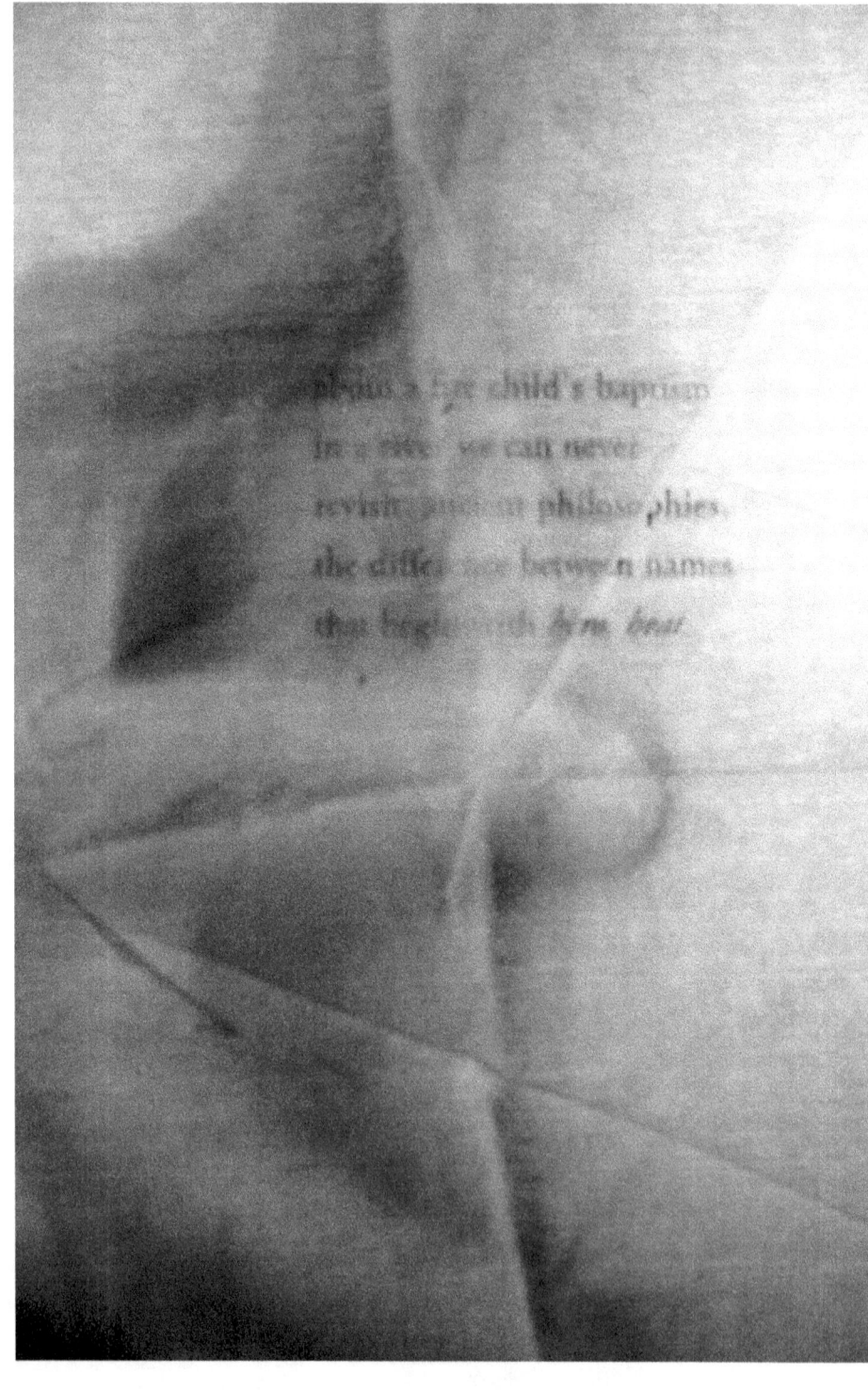

THERE IS A STORY

There is a story in all this blitz
of sound—movies, video *à clef*,
recorded books, the grainy
lilt of Tennyson's own voice reciting
the Charge of the Light Brigade—
and in the blue yarn I keep
silently feeding through my fingers
making a cloak beribboned
and fantastical to enfold
and warm my aging body
through the earth's slow
revolve into a new
equilibrium. Something
about a fire child's baptism
in a river we can never
revisit, ancient philosophies,
the difference between names
that begin with *hero, heat.*

DEATH WATCHES

You are thinner than when
I met you. You've buffed up
to celebrate sixty-three.
Today you're modeling
your only black suit
because your younger brother
is dying. His blood refuses
to stay in his arteries
or veins, instead invades
intestine, rectum, lung.
He's not the only one.

The father of a close friend,
Warren, ninety-two, is in ICU
with stomach bleeding,
a brain dementingly deprived
of the same, so today
is never going to stay with him,
so the idea of dying
has no more home in his mind
than in your brother's,
whose poignant *idée fixe*
is that you in your baggy, mildewed
suit are part of an elite
leftist conspiracy whose sole
purpose is to supplant him
in your parents' estimation.

At the very same moment you are
modeling for me, Sharif,
seventy-two, spits out what look like

coffee grounds. We've all lost count
of the number of hospitalizations
he's had this year, for heart attack,
bypass, skin ulcer, gangrene,
amputation. He rejoices in his new
prosthesis, wants to get out
of his hospital bed, slip back
into his new stride.

In an intimate anniversary embrace,
I whisper, *I have no more
unfinished business. It's hard not to
interpret this as a death wish.*
But it frees me to watch you swimming
helplessly in your unused black suit,
as if you were the one
who knew homelessness, jail,
teeth eaten away by meth,
legs engorged by cancerous
lymph, a brain made
fantastical and unforgiving
by HIV and real rivalry.
Don't go yet, I tell you. Don't divide
your parents' attention. Let him be.

Absolved now by a priest and securely
embraced by his own denial,
let him be until he can't be anymore
what he's always wanted to be—
the one bright shining star, the beacon
of his own existence.

WE WAIT TO BE SAVED

We wait to be saved
by a turn of phrase,
a gesture. This morning
in winter, seaside,
sun struck, the waves unroll
for miles inside my head.
Human voices, pure sound, weave
in, out, and press equally far
in the other direction. The wind
wraps around me, sweet
epicenter. A dozen years
we murmur, entering a peace
so sure, so cellular, I can't believe
we ever considered using words
to secure it. Beside the path
a small rabbit nestles under palmetto
fearlessly nibbling grass. A pelican
arches into the sky, dives
headlong into the shallow surf.
Two dolphins rise, submerge,
in perfect oscillation.

I want to believe we've arrived
at the epicenter of our life together,
that we have come to a point
of perfect equipoise
and that we can stay here
forever, in this peace

so sure, so cellular we know
we could never dream it up
alone. I want to believe
it will be there when all the names
are gone, when our faces are no more
familiar than the newly risen moon,
but equally desirable.

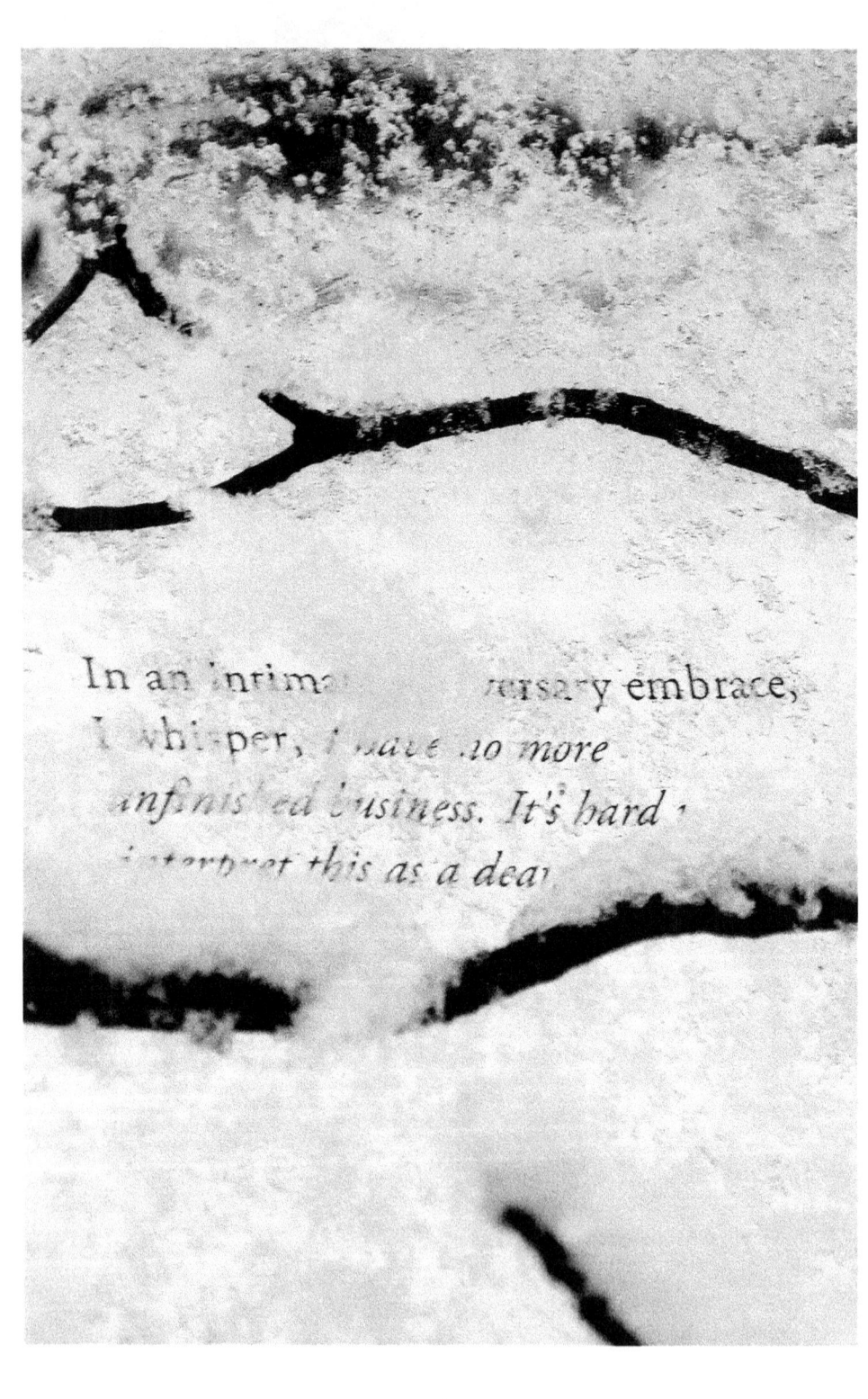

ACKNOWLEDGEMENTS

Poems in this collection were originally published in the following periodicals and anthologies:

"Lapsed Sonnet" in *Calliope*; "Glossary" in *Cardinal*; "Home Preserves" in *Fine Madness*; "Still Water" in *Greensboro Review*; "Faith" (in modified form), "Once My Mother Knew My Name", "Skin Deep", and "The Intelligence of Loss" in *Illness & Grace, Terror & Transformation*; "Sandstone" in *Intro 11*; "Attendants" in *Mid-American Review*; "Incidence" in *Montana Gothic*; "Jars" in *The Nation*; "Reification" in *Pequod*; "Clemency,""Gallery," "January, 1978," "Maple Seeds, "Martinique," "Membranes," "Objective Correlatives," "Sundew," "The Fountain," "They Know," and "Wind" in *Small Pond*; "Birdnesters," "Brandywine," "Heaven," "Tonight," "Waltz," and "Woman Devoured by Fishes" in *Southern Poetry Review*; "Il N'est Pire Aveugle Que Celui Qui Ne Veut Pas Voir" in *Southern Review*; "Flux" in *Wind*; "Can't We Just Be Happy" in *Windsor Review*; "Entre L'Arbre Et L'Écorce Il Ne Faut Pas Mettre Le Doigt," "Snow White Rose" and "Sportsmanship" in *Zone 3*. "Brandywine," "Gallery," and "Tonight" reprinted in *Anthology of Magazine Verse and Yearbook of American Poetry*; "Sandstone" reprinted in *Family Violence*, "Cicatrices," "Jars," "Spellbound," and "Reification," The Nation/Discovery prize.

Photographs are by Heather Tosteson.

Matthew Bishop provided invaluable assistance in all stages of the editing and production of this book.

There is no track. The proof of time
then is in the turning back itself.
The pull of space which realigns
is not a memory. Stranded kelp
spreads under wet red leaves before us
where we may or may not have been.

TITLE INDEX

Absent-Mindedness	221
Así Es	154
Attachment	191
Attendants	25
Augury, Omen	211
Birdnesters	68
Blossom	39
Brandywine	84
Brown Recluse	208
Burdens	226
Can't We Just Be Happy?	10
Cicatrices	114
Civics	31
Clemency	46
Cryptic	119
Death Watches	232
Dialects	26
El Día de Los Muertos	100
Entre L'Arbre et L'Écorce Il ne Faut Pas Mettre Le Doigt	86
Faith	168
Flight	212
Flux	7
Fortunes	223
Glossary	54
Heaven	78
Home Preserves	9
I Am Waiting	196
I Have Stumbled on Something	104
I See Death in My Future	215
If the Image of the Divine in Us Is Our Desire	109

Il N'est Pire Aveugle Que Celui Qui Ne Veut Pas Voir	82
Incidence	3
It Is What It Is	228
January, 1978	28
Jars	116
Koan for My Son at Twenty-One	149
La Onda	102
Lapsed Sonnet	21
Levin at Fourteen	94
Lexicon	159
Like Blood in the Vena Cava	204
Maple Seeds	13
Martinique	61
Membranes	58
Migraine	43
Mill Street	24
Objective Correlatives	52
Once My Mother Knew My Name	138
Passiflora	6
Reasonable Expectations	220
Reification	124
Sandstone	36
Shoulder to Shoulder	203
Sin Titulo	197
Skin Deep	143
Snow White Rose	76
Some Silences Are Like Silk	198
Sometimes This Does Not Feel Like Love	165
Sotano	92
Soul House	156
Spellbound	122
Sportsmanship	71
Still Water	19
Sundew	14
Teresa	65

The Call	148
The Fountain	16
The Intelligence of Loss	140
The Martyr	34
The Sanctity of the Moment	193
There Is a Moment Deep in the Night	200
There Is A Story	231
They Know	64
This Is the Flower	107
To Welcome Me, You Paint the Walls White	90
Tonight	18
Waltz	8
We Wait to Be Saved	234
Wind	48
Woman Devoured by Fishes	96

HEATHER TOSTESON, a writer, visual artist and spiritual director, has received a Nation/Discovery prize for her poetry and fellowships for poetry, fiction, and photography from MacDowell, Yaddo, the Virginia Center for the Arts, and Hambidge Center for the Creative Arts and Sciences. Her poetry, stories, and essays have appeared in numerous literary magazines. She is the author of *Visible Signs, Hearts as Big as Fists,* and *God Speaks My Language, Can You?* She holds a B.A. from Sarah Lawrence College, M.F.A. in Creative Writing from the University of North Carolina at Greensboro, and Ph.D. in English and Creative Writing from Ohio University.

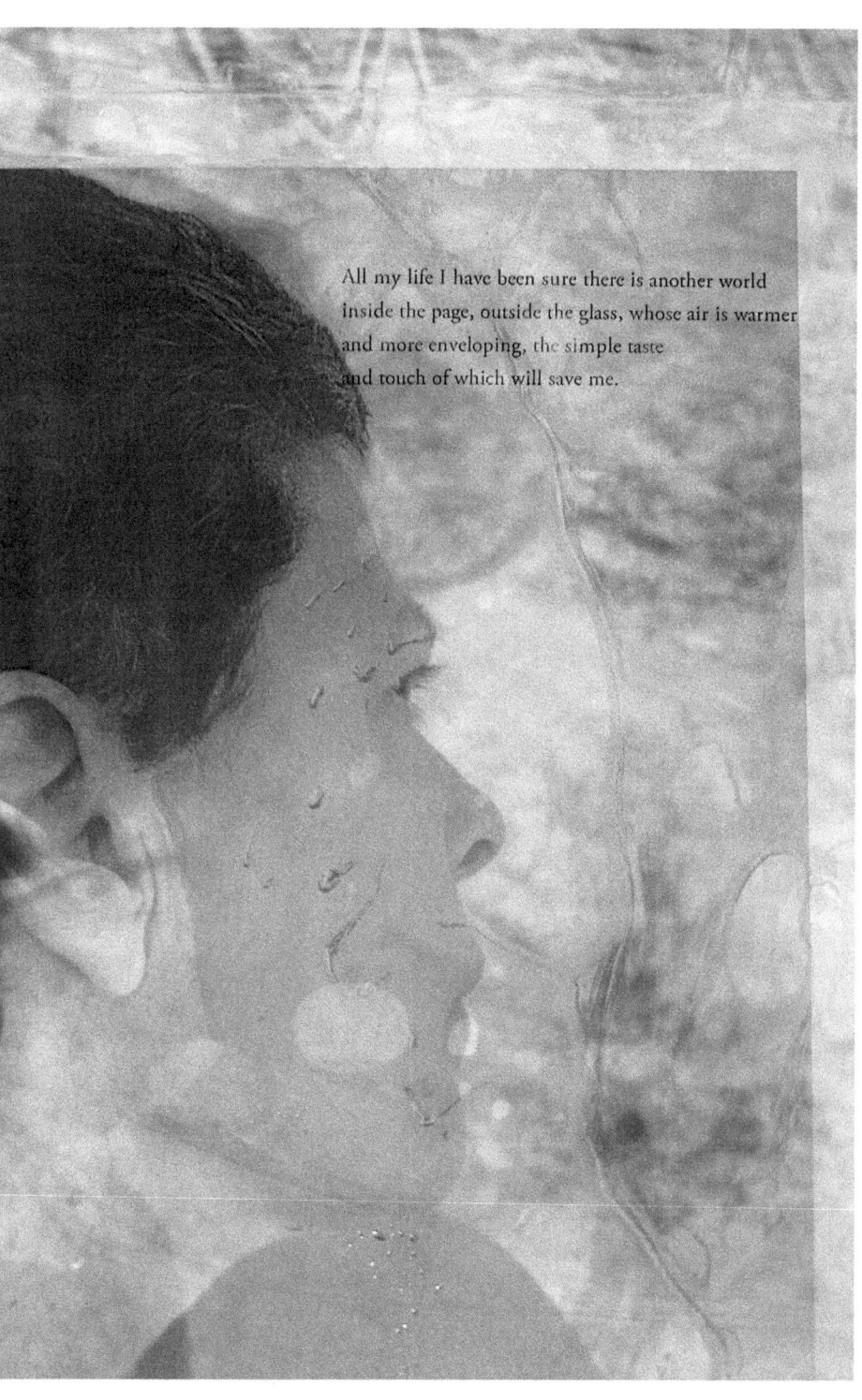

All my life I have been sure there is another world
inside the page, outside the glass, whose air is warmer
and more enveloping, the simple taste
and touch of which will save me.

www.ingramcontent.com/pod-product-compliance
Lightning Source LLC
Chambersburg PA
CBHW070641160426
43194CB00009B/1529